Defending the Ground

B (Ballymacarrett) Company
2nd Battalion 1st Belfast Brigade
3rd Northern Division
Irish Republican Army
1920 - 1922

Seán O'Coinn

Short Strand Community Tourism & Heritage Initiative © 2017

Acknowledgment

I would like to acknowledge the following:

Short Strand Community Forum-[Tourism & Heritage Initiative]

Belfast Cultural & local History Group

PRONI

Belfast Newspaper Library Archive

Bureau of Military History [Statements] Dublin

Military Archives, Dublin.

University College Dublin Archive

Belfast Cultural &Local History Group Archive

SOURCES:

Manus O Boyle Statement - Bureau of Military History

Tom Fitzpatrick Statement - Bureau of Military History

Sean Montgomery Statement - Bureau of Military History

Seamus Mc Kenna Statement-Bureau of Military History

Alf Cotton Statement - Bureau of Military History

John Quilty Statement- Bureau of Military History

Colm O'Lochlainn Statement-Bureau of Military History

Rodger McCorley recollections

Seamus Woods's papers

Sean Cunningham papers – PRONI

William Murray papers

Ernest Blythe papers -   University College Dublin

Richard Mulcahy papers - University College Dublin

Home Affairs papers - PRONI

The majority of the research carried out on the period 1920-1922 contained in this booklet was originally carried out between 1997-1999 and is held in the archive of the Belfast Cultural & Local History Group.   Seán O'Coinn   Copyright 1999/ 2017.

I would also like to thank Dessie, Frankie & Bernie for their time and commitment to this publication. Thanks also to Bernie Murray for access to her Grandfather's papers.

INTRODUCTION

It was twenty years ago that I got my first insight into the turbulent period of 1920-1922 in Belfast. I had been engaged in a project centred on a brief history of conflict in Ballymacarrett and it was the local newspaper archive that first captured my interest with its daily accounts of intense fighting in *"The East End"* It was, as one newspaper described it: *The most dangerous place in Belfast.*

Weekly reports described the gun-battles and street fighting in Ballymacarrett in streets that were more than familiar to me and at times I was intrigued at the similarities of the gun-battles of the twenties to the later battles in 1971 and 1972 which occurred in and around the Short Strand area between the IRA and the British Army. The similarities were stark. It was as if events had been captivated into a time chasm and let loose after a fifty year time span.

After all, these were the same houses, the same street corners of 50 years previous, the only difference being that the Northern state was reeling toward its conclusion of power and the" *Protestant Parliament for a Protestant people"* was close to being dissolved. It would be many years before the imbedded root and power of discrimination would be finally dislodged.

However in 1921, the Northern state was in its infancy and the Unionist power bloc had control of industry, policing and justice.

Reading through the accounts, my curiosity grew as to who these I.R.A. volunteers of 1921 were fighting to ensure the very survival of the Nationalist streets and the parish of Ballymacarrett.

Could I identify them or put a name to the volunteer in the cloth cap armed with a small service revolver or a mills bomb? Who were these men who manned the street corners and entries 50 years previous amid the *"turbulent troubles of the twenties"*. It was these questions that would stay with me, even when over the years, other commitments and work led me away from my research of the *twenties* period.

My subsequent research identified that some were former soldiers who had served in the British Army during WW1 but not all of these had enlisted in the local I.R.A. Company. However, they were still active participants in the armed defence of the district. Primary sources and records were limited and many of those who had participated had died over the passing years. So, scraping together any records I could accumulate from visits to Military Archives or U.C.D. not only gave me an intense feeling of satisfaction but also a feeling of achievement. When I managed to obtain an oral account of the period copied on to cassette tapes, by way of a friend, of Rodger Mc

Corley, a senior figure in the Belfast Brigade, it was like *mana from heaven* - a gold nugget of primary material to draw from.

This was before the power of the internet: information at the touch of a button was not available then. Unlike the recent conflict, books on the period in Belfast were literally, non-existent and none at all on the 3rd Northern Division and their role during the 1920-1922 periods. This was is in stark contrast to the books that filled my bookcase written of those who fought in the south of the country: the Flying Columns of Cork, Mayo and Tipperary, the legendary actions of Michael Collins in Dublin and the autobiographies of figures such as Dan Breen, Ernie O'Malley and Tom Barry.

I began to think of the 3rd Northern Division as hidden within the national shadow, *deliberately hidden* as not to create a link between *"the old I.R.A."* and the modern day I.R.A. raging a similar guerrilla war in the north.

But, it goes a bit deeper than that and much of the explanation lays within the underhand politics of the period and the betrayal and abandonment of the Northern I.R.A. by the Provisional government in 1922.

Volunteers were left in a hostile environment and had to join the Free State Amy, emigrate, or simply filter back into community life in Belfast, but always on the watch list of the Northern authorities who had interned many republicans up until December 1924 and there after if they felt the need to do so.

Stories of involvement in the twenties were kept to private gatherings of old comrades, or tales of various actions, talked about at wakes with the passing of an old comrade. There were no graphic publications on *"their fight for Irish Freedom "*

In the early period of my research, I came across Jimmy Mc Dermott, who was working on a history of the 3rd Northern Division. Our paths of research crossed and I also gave him a copy of the Mc Corley tapes.

While I was drawn in other directions of research and other commitments overtook my time, I was delighted that Jimmy Mc Dermott's book:

Northern Divisions: *The Old I.R.A. and the Belfast Pogroms* 1920-22, was published in 2001.

Other books began to follow, including Robert Lynch's *The Northern I.R.A. and the Early Years of Partition* 1920-1922 - (2006) and Alan Parkinson's book: *Belfast's Unholy War*- [Dublin 2004]

More ground breaking was that the Bureau of Military History in Dublin opened up witness statements given by veterans in the 1940s and 1950s.

In more recent times another book analysing the role of the Belfast I.R.A. during the 1920-1922 periods was written by Kieran Glennon, whose Grandfather had been an officer in the 3rd Northern Division and following the truce, the Free State Army.

Kieran's book: *From Pogrom to Civil War Tom Glennon and the Belfast I.R.A.* was published in 2013 and provides a well-researched overview of the period.

Although from Dublin, Kieran has a direct connection to St. Matthews, in that his Great Grandparents were married in the church on the 28th August, 1893.

My reason for returning to this story came about due to the recent centenary commemorations around the First World War and the Easter Rising.

For republicans myself included, the Easter rising was the primary event of commemoration, but for me personally, I was also equally aware that within my own community, there was a number of men who had fought and died during WW1 and I took the challenging decision to not only begin researching these men in more detail, but to also produce a publication on them.

The uniform they wore did not change their names, or the streets they originated from, or the fact they were an integral part of the history of Nationalist Ballymacarrett.

When they enlisted to fight in a world conflict, there was no British occupation of their streets and in the main during the war years of 1914-1918, *Nationalism*, rather than Republicanism, would have been very much within the political thinking of the population.

Economics was also a driving factor.

History had forgotten these men; they had become trapped in a flawed and distorted manner of how the dead of WW1 were remembered in the north. Unionism made it *"their history"*; even the poppy wrongly became a Unionist symbol in the north.

The British occupation of Ireland, the struggle for independence, partition and the creation of a Unionist state in the north-east of the country, all combined to condemn Nationalist war dead to the doldrums of history.

Yet, within communities such as Ballymacarrett/Short Strand, when men returned from the horrific carnage of that war, they faced the same religious and economic discrimination of their neighbours.

For some, their military experience was put to use when the fighting began on the streets of Belfast in 1920. While a number joined the I.R.A., others did not, but were active in defending their community.

The role played by Catholic ex-servicemen has been downplayed.

There is no argument in the fact many joined the Free State Army in 1922, but equally Republicans also joined the Free State Army, as options for employment, especially in the six counties, were not overflowing with choice.

Seamus Woods, the O/C of the 3rd Northern Division stated that:

> *"When the pogrom started the Catholics organised in their own areas and a defence force had to be organised, so we took in the ex-soldiers to the Irish Volunteers "*

Tom McNally, Quartermaster of the Belfast Brigade and a fierce opponent of the A.O.H., also remarked:

"The only men to rely on were the Irish Volunteers and some of the ex-servicemen."

B Company, 2nd Battalion, 1st Belfast Brigade was raised in 1920 to counter the attacks being made against the Nationalist quarter of Ballymacarrett and parish of St. Matthew's.

It comprised of an initial strength of 120 men, many unemployed and was firstly commanded by a Donegal man, Manus O' Boyle and later by John, (Sean) Cunningham from Comber Street a former regular soldier in the British Army. Along with Manus O Boyle, Sean Cunningham was responsible for raising the Company.

Over the next two years they would be engaged in some of the worst fighting on the streets of Belfast against overwhelming odds and a state endorsed pogrom against Nationalist districts.

Unfortunately, as very few primary records exist, detailing a comprehensive account of Company actions, is not possible and the roles played by the ordinary volunteers, have been lost to history.

However, for the first time, that curiosity that first gripped me sitting in the Newspaper library in Belfast, 20 years ago, can at least be partly fulfilled, as this book will list the nominal role of B Company in full-{both as at and after the truce period of July 1921]

Names can be put to those volunteers who fought on the streets of Ballymacarrett, during one of the most crucial periods in the history of St. Matthew's parish.

For this reason publications such as this are historically important within a community context. History stems from the grassroots and communities need to take empowerment and ownership of THEIR history.

We are in an age of revisionism especially within academia, so as we enter into the centenary periods of the War of Independence and the creation of the northern state, it is imperative that communities retain empowerment over what after all, *is their history.*

> *Seán O'Coinn*   *Ballymacarrett*   **JUNE 2017**

POLITICAL BACKGROUND TO THE OUTBREAK OF WAR.

Edwardian Belfast was a city of sectarian ethnocentrism, where the politics of "Home Rule" or maintaining the Union with Britain overshadowed the common need of working class politics in an economic sense.

Within Unionism, the reinvigorated advancement of Catholic Nationalism sparked sectarian propaganda, fear and suspicion, with animosity again coming to the fore. It was fuelled mainly by the Unionist business class who not only held sway over economic life in the city, but also influenced thinking among the majority of working class Protestants who struggled to survive in the same small Victorian houses that formed the tightly bound streets and lanes of Industrial Belfast, as their Catholic neighbours.

Unionist insecurity led them to foster a systematic policy of discrimination against Catholic workers and they endeavoured to ensure that well paid, skilled trades remained in Protestant hands. Despite this however, the national revival of Irish culture, identity and the Home Rule campaign being intensified at Westminster, saw Belfast's Catholics begin to assert themselves. A strong base of political outreach linked with social opportunity was taking shape in order to break the Unionist grip.

The Catholic claim to political expression and social opportunity within the city of Belfast had been already boosted when the Unionist-controlled Belfast Corporation in City Hall, was forced to accept two Catholic wards within the extended city in 1896.

But it was the issue of Home Rule that sparked most fear within Unionism and from that emerged a determined resistance mainly within their strong base of Ulster which they considered solidly and homogeneously Unionist. This policy of resistance was to have its political stance supported by a newly formed group in January 1913 called the Ulster Volunteer Force [U.V.F.] created to oppose Home Rule. [A group already existed within Belfast Unionism with the same purpose known as the Belfast Protestant Association]

This move by Unionists was countered by a similar Nationalist force, the Irish Volunteers, also referred to as the "Irish National Volunteers" [after the split and the outbreak of war in 1914]. The Irish Volunteers established itself throughout the island of Ireland.

The military element of Unionism and their over confidence of holding Ulster had a catalytic effect on the growth of the Irish Volunteers in the north as it incensed Nationalists of the western counties. In March 1914, branches of the Nationalist force were established throughout counties Tyrone, Fermanagh and Derry, while in Belfast some 150 members were enrolled. [By October 1914, the Belfast membership would rise to 3,200 men]. Overall in the north, the new organization increased at a phenomenal rate and by May 1914 of the 129,000 Irish Volunteers throughout Ireland, 41,000 were enrolled in Ulster, including some 18,000 in counties Tyrone, Derry and Donegal. Both of the opposing sides had now created Citizen Armies, a fact not lost on a British cabinet looking at putting the country on a war footing following the outbreak of war in Europe in August 1914. The two main British political parties, the Liberals and the Conservatives entered into a "party truce" in the face of "External Danger". This left the still unresolved "Irish Question" in a state of suspended animation. Britain now worked the Irish Problem to its advantage, promising both sides a positive outcome at the war's end in return for their support for the war effort.

This was forthcoming from both leaders of the two opposing sides, Redmond and Carson. Carson's U.V.F. was quick to rally to the colours when called to do so.

The adventure of war, escape from poor social conditions and loyalty to the British Crown made it very easy for Britain to recruit these organized semi-trained volunteer armies. But Redmond's task was an invidious one: he had to demonstrate the loyalty of Nationalists in the crisis whilst maintaining his party's supremacy in Irish politics so that he might win the most favourable settlement of the Ulster question after the war.

But the imperially-minded Redmond seriously miscalculated the opinion at home and his British recruitment policy precipitated a split in the Volunteers.

With political tensions growing within the leadership, Redmond held a meeting in Dublin City Hall on Wednesday 30th September 1914, at which he created what was now termed the Irish National Volunteers.

Support for the new "Nationalist Volunteers" was overwhelming in Belfast, among the volunteer companies including E Company East Belfast, 2nd Battalion.

Nine volunteer companies across the city sided with Redmond and in a packed meeting of the Belfast Volunteers held on Sunday 4th October 1914 in St. Mary's Hall, Bank Street, a motion by Joseph Devlin, MP for West Belfast, to affiliate into the Nationalist Volunteer Movement, was adopted.

Eddie McNeff *a volunteer of E Company 2nd Battalion, who was killed during Easter Week, 1916 in the Battle of Hulluch while serving with the 8th Battalion, Iniskilling Fusiliers*

Twelve days later on Friday 16th October, the first delegate meeting of the Belfast Regiment of the new National Volunteers met in St. Mary's Hall and Joseph Devlin was elected President.

Those who opposed Redmond and Devlin now designated themselves the Irish Volunteers, later known as Óglaigh na hÉireann [Volunteers of Ireland] and although their numbers were small, the split marked the end of the National Volunteers as an effective force in the north. Redmond still held the majority of support within the Volunteer Movement, which reflected that most Nationalists even in the north hoped his policy of supporting Britain's war effort might succeed in delivering a settlement, which would prevent permanent partition.

With Irishmen signing up in their thousands to fight, the Nationalist Volunteers fell into decline. By the early months of 1916, it had ceased route marches and military activity. A decisive factor in Belfast was the enlistment in the Royal Navy of the Belfast regiment's commander, Doctor Hugh McNally, later killed with Lord Kitchener in the sinking of *HMS Hampshire.*

The view of Anglo-Irishman G.F.H. Berkeley is important to note. He acted as organiser of the Volunteer Movement in Belfast in 1914 and had the distinct impression that the Home Rule leaders wished to "let the Volunteers cease to exist in the north-east since they rather feared disturbance amongst the Nationalists in the event of their exclusion from Home Rule" *"Devlin"*, he records*," had aroused resentment amongst the local Volunteers over his reluctance to provide them* with weapons". Many of the 800 rifles obtained by Devlin for Belfast were as Berkeley described *"Of a strange foreign bore, which were hard to get ammunition for".*

By the end of 1915 there was a degree of apathy toward the Nationalist Volunteers. Unlike the U.V.F. who enjoyed the support of the Orange Order, the I.N.V. in areas such as Tyrone for example found only limited support from the Hibernians. Thousands of the rank and file had marched off to war against Germany and the politics of war left Ireland much in the background.

Nationalist influence at Westminster decreased in importance, yet despite the establishment of a Coalition Government in May 1915, which included Unionists, Redmond continued to call for recruits. It now appeared that Unionism had acquired a dominating influence in a government where the future of the Home Rule Act depended upon that government's goodwill.

The Belfast National Volunteers remained in existence until October 1918 when what was considered its remaining weapons-210 rifles of Old Italian pattern....in bad condition were handed over to the British military.   [In 1920, 60 I.N.V. rifles found their way into the hands of the Belfast I.R.A.]

Redmond's reputation was now flawed and events of Easter 1916 in Dublin would mark the beginning of the end for his Nationalist Party and its pro-British policy. The revolutionary Republican Movement struck a blow against British forces in Dublin in what became a *"blood sacrifice"*. It was originally conceived by the Irish Republican Brotherhood –IRB, as a national revolt. But with the struggle effectively contained to Dublin, the theme of sacrifice became paramount. *"Military failure turned to martyrdom as the British engaged in harsh retribution"*.

The Easter Rising had initially engendered feelings of bafflement, verging on hostility, but the execution of sixteen of the leaders over a period of ten days, together with the mass arrest of 3,400 Sinn Fein activists and sympathizers, induced a sea of change in Irish public opinion as condemnation of the rebels turned to resentment of their treatment.

CHARLIE MONAHAN AND THE AUD 1916

For the rising to succeed, plans had been put in place to land thousands of rifles in Ireland to arm the volunteers throughout the country.

Arrangements for the cargo of twenty thousand rifles and a million rounds of ammunition had been made in the United States between John Devoy, head of

Clan- na- Gael in the United States and Herr von Skal, a member of the staff at the German Embassy in Washington. [Clan-na-Gael had been founded in 1867 as the United States wing of the Irish Republican Brotherhood]

The *Aud*, a German vessel flying a Norwegian flag was to off-load her cargo of twenty thousand rifles captured from the Russians by the Germans, into small Irish ships in the Bay of Tralee.

However, owing to difficulties in communication, or because there was some misunderstanding about the time the *Aud* was to arrive, no one was there to receive her signal when she arrived off the Irish coast.

That job had been assigned to seven volunteers that included Charlie Monaghan of the Dublin Brigade, Con Keating, Don Sheehan and Tom Mc Inerney from Limerick.

The four men never reached their destination as the car in which they were travelling, took a wrong turning and ran off the narrow dark road leading to *Balllykisan* and crashed near the Pier killing three of those on board on *Good Friday* night, 23rd April 1916.

Only Tom McInerney the driver of the car survived the fatal crash.

The *Aud* was apprehended by British naval sloops, but while being escorted into Queenstown Harbour, the ship scuttled herself and the rifles. All the ammunition along with ten machine-guns, went down with her.

Charlie Monaghan [MONAHAN] was born in Belfast on the 21st March 1879. He was one of three sons of Robert Monahan a Wood Cutting Machinists by trade and a prominent member of The Irish National Forrester's. The

Charlie Monaghan [MONAHAN]

organization was formed in Dublin in 1877, with a Belfast branch being established in 1882. Several members also held membership of the IRB-Irish Republican Brotherhood.

The family lived in a small lane type street at No. 23 Riley's Place, off Cromac Street and Charlie attended the Christian Brothers School in Oxford Street.

He moved to Dublin in 1900 and immigrated to the United States in 1914, before returning to Dublin less than two years later, where he had family connections that included his sister, brother-in-law and his uncle John.

He joined the Volunteers and it was his experience of working with electronic communications that found him on that ill-fated journey along a narrow Kerry road during Easter week of 1916.

Charlie Monahan's body was only recovered from the River *Laune* on the 30th October, six months after his tragic death. His remains were buried two days later in Drumavally churchyard, Killorglin along with Don Sheehan.

AILBHE Ó MONACHÁIN
Uachtarán, Oireachtas na Gaeilge

His younger brother, Alfred-[Ailbhe] was also active in the volunteers and fought in the west of the country. Born on the 25th January 1889, he joined the volunteers in 1914. Ailbhe was instructed to go to Galway and assist Liam Mellows in organising the rising in the west. He remained there during the War of Independence and following the truce he took the anti-treaty side during the civil war and continued to serve alongside Liam Mellows who was executed by Free State Forces.

Alfred was a *gaelgoir* and became a school teacher, before dying on 30th July 1967. He is buried in Saint Colmcille's Swords, County Dublin.

His Father, Robert who died in February 1908, was buried in Milltown Cemetery on the 23rd February, 1908.

In relation to the ill-fated episode of the *Aud*, the Vice Commandant of the Tralee Battalion and Adjutant to the Kerry Brigade of the Volunteers, **Alf Cotton**, gave a very interesting statement on the incident.

In his own written testament of the rising, Alf Cotton stated that he had intended on *Good Friday*, for a small, but effective armed force of volunteers to be encamped in the Banna area close to Fenit Pier to protect the landing of the weapons and also Sir Rodger Casement, who would be put ashore from a German submarine.

However, Cotton went on to explain: "*this intention was not carried out, for on a visit to Belfast in March 1916, he was served with an order under the* **Defence of the Realm Act** *forbidding him to return to the counties of Cork and Kerry and confining him strictly to the City of Belfast*".

Cotton said that: "*he had planned on ignoring the exclusion order but that*

Sean Mc Dermott-[Sean Mac Diarmada] was afraid that his presence in Kerry would endanger the arms landing".

"*I was told during a visit to Dublin, to return to Belfast and sever all connections with Kerry until the rising was over*"

He also recalled that: "**Mc Dermott did not like the idea of a small camp being set up at Banna to coincide with the proposed landing of the weapons**".

Another interesting comment made by Alf Cotton relates to how Bulmer Hobson had several heated arguments with Pearse over the rising.

Cotton accounted: "**Hobson [with whom I was friendly] was opposed to plans for a rising, which Pearse entertained. He [Hobson] wanted a fight conducted on guerrilla tactics and he was largely responsible for that during training.**

Hobson told me that he and Pearse had heated arguments about the matter.

On one occasion Pearse had admitted that he could not deny the soundness of Hobson's arguments, but stated that we "must have a sacrifice".

Hobson's main argument was that gambling everything in one throw was not good tactics and that the adoption of guerrilla fighting would enable us to make a more sustained effort with better prospects of success."

Bulmer Hobson

Bulmer Hobson a Quaker and printer by trade, was born on 14th January, 1883. His family lived at 24 Hopefield Avenue, Antrim Road, Belfast.

A member of the Gaelic League, he was a founding member along with David Parkhill and Joseph Campbell from East Belfast, of the **Ulster Literary Theatre** in Clarence Place.

On the 26 June, 1902, he established the republican scouting organization **Na Fianna Eireann** and the first *Sluagh*-[branch] was *Sluagh Clann Rudhraigh.*

Hobson became a member of the IRB in 1904 and was a founder member of the **Dungannon Clubs** in March 1905.

Working along with Denis McCullough, the Dungannon Clubs formed an association with the separatist movement **Cumann nGaedheal** established by Arthur Griffith in the south to foster the idea of Irish identity and self-reliance.

Out of the fusion of the two groups in April 1907, came Sinn Fein- not, at this stage, a political creed, but indicative rather of an attitude.

As the translation of the words suggests, Irishmen were being urged to rely on themselves and no one else.

Hobson and McCullough would later leave Sinn Fein and they established a new organization in May 1912 called **The Freedom Club**. They first met on the 7th June 1912 and was a front for the IRB. The club was also responsible for the initial formation of the Irish Volunteers in Belfast.

The loss of the weapons from the *Aud* restricted the rising mainly to Dublin and spelt its ultimate failure from a military standpoint. It was originally conceived by the IRB as a National Revolt, but with the struggle effectively narrowed to the capital, the theme of sacrifice became paramount.

Hobson's view of a guerrilla war was indeed correct, but may have been a few years ahead of its time as the support was not there among the general populace.

When Michael Collins implemented the same thinking some three years later, the mood of the people had changed in favour of republicanism.

Pearse got *his blood sacrifice* and with it came a growing base of support for revolution in Ireland.

Military failure turned to martyrdom as the British engaged in harsh retribution.

In the aftermath of the rising, Dublin was a city confused, desperate and full of rumours. As a consequence of the rising, 1,351 people were killed, seriously wounded, or maimed. 179 buildings in the centre of the city were either destroyed or gutted by fire.

A memorial, erected in April 1939 now stands at Ballykisan Pier for Charlie Monahan, Con Keating and Don Sheehan.

The release of prisoners from the rising in 1918 saw a new tide of passion sweep Ireland in favour of Sinn Fein. Throughout the latter half of 1917, Sinn Fein clubs spread through the northern counties as the younger generation looked to the attainment of Independence without partition.

The concept of partition was first muted by British Prime Minister, Lloyd George following the rising, when he voiced the idea of Home Rule in Ireland, with the exception of the six north-eastern counties, which would be "temporarily" placed under a Provisional government led by Edward Carson.

The Irish Parliamentary Party, accepted the proposal after a stormy conference lasting five hours, took place in St.Mary's Hall in Belfast on the 23rd June, 1916

.It proved to be a watershed in northern Nationalist politics as Sinn Fein bitterly opposed the decision and the split in Nationalism became complete.

Two years later, the 1918 general elections saw Sinn Fein eclipse the IPP, winning 73 seats, leaving the IPP with only 6- [5 of which were from the 9 seats in Ulster] having lost 62 seats.

Sinn Fein was now the motive power in Nationalist Ireland.

The Sinn Fein party abstained from the British parliament at Westminster and set up **Dail Eireann** in Dublin. In their eyes and in that of the majority of the people of Ireland, *An Dail*, was now the governing body of Ireland, with, or without British recognition.

It was far from being a fully functioning government, but it did represent a striking way of questioning British legitimacy in Ireland,

It composed the elected representatives of the Irish nation and the only authority in Ireland with the moral sanction of a democracy behind it.

Sinn Fein had fought the election led by Eamon de Valera asserting the inalienable right of Ireland to self-determination and sovereign independence and declared the intention of appealing to the Versailles Peace Conference on these grounds.

Ireland had declared that it would make use of *"any and every means available to render impotent the power of England to hold Ireland in subjection by military force or otherwise".*

The *Aud.*

BACKGROUND TO THE FATAL OPERATION OF 23rd APRIL 1916, WHICH RESULTED IN THE DEATHS OF VOLUNTEERS CHARLIE MONAGHAN, CON KEATING AND DONAL SHEEHAN.

A week prior to the rising, five volunteers of the Wireless Section of the Volunteers gathered at the small *Munster Hotel* owned by staunch Kerry republican Myra T Mc Carthy at 44 Mountjoy Street in Dublin.

They were there to be briefed by Sean Mc Dermott on an operation to take place at Caherciveen, County Kerry, three days before the rising was to commence.

Present at the briefing was:

Denis Daly, Charlie Monaghan, Donal Sheehan, Colm O'Lochlainn and Con Keating.

The "*Job*" set for the men entailed them travelling by train from Dublin to Killarney from were they would precede by cars to the Maurice Fitzgerald Wireless College at Caherciveen and remove two radio transmitters before destroying by fire the room from were the transmitters had been removed.

The dismantling of the two transmitters was to be overseen by Con Keating a skilled Wireless Operator. They would then make contact with Austin Stack at 5am early the following morning in Tralee.

Upon contact in Tralee they would set up one of the transmitters at J P O Donnell's home at Ballyard Road and make contact with the *Aud*.

That done, the two radio transmitters were to be moved out of the area by Austin Stack; one to Limerick and the other to Athenry.

The radio transmitters were then to be used to broadcast the news of the rising.

The five volunteers would then return to Dublin by train from Killarney.

On the morning of 23rd April 1916, "*Good Friday*", the five men were to pick up their tickets from an IRB man at the Ballast office of Kingsbridge Station and board the early mail train to Killarney.

Colm O'Lochlainn recalled the morning in Dublin and that the IRB contact was Michael Collins who passed over their tickets. It was a brief encounter, with Collin's saying, "*you have your orders*" Colm who arrived at the meeting point on his trusted Lucania cyclic, handed it over to Mick Collins. He later enquired after it and Collin's in true nature told him that *it ended up amid a barricade on Abbey Street*.

Upon arrival at Killarney, the men were met by the two cars as planned.

These had been organised in Limerick by John Quilty.

The two cars were an American Brisco, owned by John Quilty, but with false number plates and a Maxwell.

Tom Mc Inerney was the driver of the Brisco and Sam Windrum the Maxwell.

[Sam Windrum, picked by John Quilty for the job, had been sworn into the Volunteers the previous night by Commandant Jim Ledden in the presence of Mc Inerney and Quilty, in order to take part in the operation]

Tom Mc Inerney took Charlie Monaghan, Con Keating and Don Sheehan, while Sam Windrum led off with Denis Daly and Colm O'Lochlainn on board.

The evening was now drawing in and fog had descended as the two cars began the journey to Cahirciveen.

En route, between Killorglin and Cahirciveen, the two cars lost sight of each other and Tom Mc Inerney stopped in Killorglin to ask a young girl called Lilly Taylor for the road to Cahirciveen; she replied *"turn left at the Chapel gate"*.

The turning that Tom Mc Inerney made in the dark was not the road, but the approach to Ballykisan Pier.

By the time he realised the error and began relaying this to the men on board, the car plunged over the pier into the river.

Three local men rushed from their cottages to try and help as Tom and Con Keating struggled to swim to the bank.

Local men Thady O Sullivan and Father and Son, Patrick and Michael Begley, endeavoured to save the two volunteers.

Tom recalled that Con went down beside him, his last words being *"Jesus, Mary and Joseph"*. He-[Tom] was fortunate to be pulled out by the Begleys and brought to Thady O Sullivan's cottage.

Meantime the other car had to abandon the mission due to an increase in RIC patrols in the area and a section of British soldiers deployed around the Wireless College. So it would appear that the British had their own intelligence of a possible raid.

Arrests later followed. Austin Stack was arrested, Tom Mc Inerney ended up in *Frongoch* and John Quilty and Sam Windrim were also arrested in Limerick.

Denis Daly and Colm O'Lochlainn made it back to Dublin by train.

Had the operation succeeded plans had been put in place for rifles from the *Aud* to be transported by train to Limerick and a supply sent down into Galway to Liam Mellows.

Limerick was also the destination for Rodger Casement were he was to stay at John Daly's in Barrington Street.

44 Mountjoy St Dublin were Charlie Monaghan and his comrades were briefed prior to the Ill - fated trip to Kerry

COGADH NA SAOIRSE, THE I.R.A. AND ATTEMPTED POGROMS.

The Nationalist party, who remained at Westminster with only six seats after the 1918 elections, believed that the abstention of the 73 Sinn Fein members would enable Carson to use a strengthened Ulster Unionist representation to press for the permanent exclusion of the six counties in any future Irish settlement.

Joseph Devlin contended that the presence of a sizable Nationalist party in the House of Commons during the 1919-21 periods might have shaped the future of the northern minority rather differently.

The Unionist press in the six counties viewed Unionist anxiety of the Dail's first meeting in the Mansion House on the 21st January 1919, with ridicule, which simply showed the absurdity of such foolish reaction

.In reality, behind the ridicule lay a realization that events in Dublin had serious implications for the future of Ireland. The claim to national self-determination in the atmosphere of 1919 was potentially a most powerful one, despite northern Unionism initial response that no Irish nation existed.

This can only be described as political naivety, which within less than a year had quickly changed.

In March 1920, the Ulster Unionist Council agreed not to oppose the new Government of Ireland Bill embodying partition and two Home Rule parliaments in Ireland. Therefore, Unionists were now more anxious to stress the distinctiveness of two Irish entities and each of their people, pursuing again the policy of a six county state.

As the Dail sat in Dublin on the 21st January, 1919, the first military action was taking place at Soloheadberg in County Tipperary.

The new **Irish Republican Army** carried out an ambush on an R.I.C. patrol, but this was the product of local initiative rather than a timely political action from any central command. In fact, at that time, the I.R.A. often acted under their own control rather than taking direction from the Dail.

It was now clear that widespread action would soon begin throughout the country. Sinn Fein had established a self-styled government with Eamon de Valera as its president and *Cogadh na Saoirse*, a guerrilla war against the British occupation of Ireland was underway. I.R.A. raids for weapons in the summer of 1919 were carried out against the Unionist "big houses" across Ireland. In the north, *Ballyedmond Castle* near Rostrevor in County Down was targeted. The estate house was the home of Major O.S Nugent, a U.V.F. leader who had died in 1914. The raid carried out in May 1919, was successful in obtaining a substantial amount of weaponry.

Three months later in August, *Drumkilly House* in Armagh was targeted without success, while guns and ammunition was landed from a fishing boat on the beach at Minerstown, County Down in January 1920.

By the end of 1919, the I.R.A. had succeeded in making it impossible for the R.I.C. to operate in the south and west of the country. Meanwhile Dail Eireann had set up a Republican infrastructure throughout Ireland.

In many areas, taxes were no longer paid to the British Exchequer and only Republican courts sat in process manned by Sinn Fein. British rule had in effect, broken down.

But the British were striking back implementing their own strategy of repression, targeting Sinn Fein and I.R.A. personnel.

On the 20th March, 1920, an R.I.C. squad shot and killed the Lord Mayor of Cork and O/C of the 1st Cork Brigade, Tomas Mac Curtain.

The *Irish Times* reported on the 1st May 1920, that the government was fighting a losing battle and the forces of the Crown were being driven back on Dublin. The King's government had virtually ceased to exist south of the Boyne and west of the Shannon. This may have been somewhat of an overstatement, but there was no doubting that British law was now being "*enforced, rather than being maintained*".

In Belfast Unionist newspapers were reporting on the 10th and 14th May, of a Sinn Fein campaign in the north against R.I.C. barracks.

The I.R.A. in Belfast had grown out of the Irish Volunteers which had begun to organise in early 1917. At this stage it was more a case of an organization, than of a fully trained body of men.

Recruits were young and inexperienced, so training from the core root was essential and continued throughout the period into 1919.

Companies were structured as follows:

A COMPANY was split into two PLATOONS with each Platoon commanded by a Lieutenant. A PLATOON was split into two sections, each with its own commander.

A SECTION was in turn split into two Squads, each with a Squad commander.

Training took place in the hills around Belfast and each Saturday evening there would be extended order drills.

By the summer of 1920, the tactics of the I.R.A. had achieved a considerable measure of success in the south despite the reinforcement of the R.I.C. by Auxiliaries, along with an increasing resort to counter-terror measures by the British authorities.

Sinn Fein dominated local government in rural Ireland.

Even in the north, Sinn Fein was making advances on the old Nationalist party.

In the council elections of June 1920, the Unionists suffered a severe setback, when counties Fermanagh and Tyrone returned anti-partitionist majorities, made up of Sinn Fein and the Nationalist party.

In South Armagh, the leader of the I.R.A.'s 4th Northern Division, headed the poll in the Nationalist division, whilst in the Unionist controlled Down County Council, Sinn Fein won 4 seats to the Nationalist parties one seat.

In the wake of these elections, a sudden outbreak of sectarian violence in Derry claimed 19 lives.

In the wake of the I.R.A. killing of R.I.C. Commissioner G.F.S Smyth, a former British Army Colonel, in County Cork, in retaliation for the killing of Tomas Mac Curtain, Loyalist rioting erupted in Banbridge, County Down.

Smyth was a native of the town and had been found to be implicated by the I.R.A. in Tomas Mc Curtain's killing along with District Inspector Oswald Swanzy.

Catholic homes and business premises were attacked, burned and wrecked by rampaging mobs. The sectarian attacks which had been exasperated by a continuous stream of vehement anti-Catholic comments and reports in the Unionist press now spread to the towns of Dromore, Lisburn and Newtownards.

Many Catholic families were forced to move into Nationalist districts of Belfast.

Smyth's body was brought north for burial in Banbridge and on the day of the funeral, 21st July, 1920, a sectarian pogrom was activated in Belfast.

A violent onslaught was made upon the Catholic employees in the Belfast Shipyard.

Serious rioting and sniping began, Catholic owned public houses were looted and homes and business premises attacked and burned.

Nineteen people were killed over the following week as the war reached Belfast with its in-trenched sectarian history.

Protestant mobs and snipers defied an indulgent police, while the British Army would at times indiscriminately sweep the streets with gunfire in order to disperse the crowds.

I.R.A. snipers did what they could in order to repel mob onslaughts in and around the Springfield/Clonard and in Ballymacarrett. The fighting at times was vicious.

An exception in regards to British Army policy over this period, occurred on the 22nd July, when Lieutenant John Woodthorpe commanding a Platoon of eighteen soldiers of the 1st Norfolk Regiment, entered the grounds of St. Matthew's and. Proceeded to drive back a large mob that were stoning the soldiers.

When shots rang out, Lieutenant Woodthorpe ordered his soldiers to open fire, killing three, two of whom were women.

At the subsequent inquest, Lieutenant Woodthorpe gave evidence.

He stated: "*About 7.30pm on the 22nd July, I saw a dense and hostile crowd around the Roman Catholic Chapel, Bryson Street.*

They were climbing the railings of the chapel. I rushed up about eighteen men and entered the Chapel grounds. They managed to clear away the crowd who were stoning the Chapel and the troops. Shots were fired and I gave the order to open fire."

The incident described by Lieutenant John Woodthorpe is one amid an afternoon of attacks upon the Church and surrounding streets, which began around 4pm as hundreds of Protestants surged down Bryson Street and began attacking homes in the Catholic streets-[Comber, Kilmood and Beechfield streets] running between Bryson Street and Seaforde Street

Desperate hand-to-hand fighting ensued, before residents rallied and forced the large mob back toward Bryson Street.

The attack was brief but vicious and was broken up by British soldiers opening fire with a Lewis machine-gun. Several bursts of gunfire was directed from Beechfield Street over the heads of both the residents and the attacking mob.

Two hours later at 6pm another sustained attack by sections of a crowd numbering upwards of two thousand strong was launched again toward the Church and the Cross and Passion Convent in Bryson Street.

Once more, the residents rallied and not only struggled to push back the large mob, but also had to rescue the frightened families sheltering in the parochial hall, who had been forced from their homes on the Newtownards Road.

They eventually succeeded in pushing back the mob and the British Army, as stated also opened fire to repel the attack.

In stark contrast the same regiment-Norfolk Regiment, swept Cupar Street and Kashmir Road in the Clonard district with gunfire as opposing crowds clashed. Women with babies fled along Cupar Street as gunfire showed no compassion in its indiscriminate bearing on the people.

The day ended with twelve dead and forty-six injured.

The following day, [23rd July] saw no let up as large crowds again gathered on the Newtownards Road. That night amid the turmoil that had engulfed the area, hundreds of Protestants broke through at the top of Bryson Street and surged toward the Church and Convent, but once again were driven back with military assistance.

British soldiers were posted at street corners in the area between Bridge End and Bryson Street. Makeshift sandbagged posts were established with barbed wire entanglements placed at Seaforde Street and Wolff Street and a temporary billet was established in part of the Labour Exchange at the junction of Short Strand and Bridge End.

The reign of terror left a pathetic sight of many homeless people wandering the streets looking for shelter. Small handcarts were used to salvage belongings. In many cases, whole families were affected, the situation made worst by the cries of distressed children. With a feeling of dispirit, they sought shelter wherever they could find it.

This was a time of poverty and survival, with no welfare state to draw on for support.

"They were in fact, refugees".

Church halls and relatives were the only option open to them, in what were already overcrowded, cramped small terrace houses. Many of these already accommodated large families and all this combined to the despair brought on by the attempted pogrom against Nationalist districts.

The military tended in general [although there were exceptions] to sweep indiscriminate gunfire into the streets as a method of simply dispersing the crowds.

This gunfire favoured no one and killed many. Of the nine people killed in Ballymacarrett in 1920 by the military, seven were Protestants, one of whom was a fifteen year old girl, shot during the disturbances around the Convent in Bryson Street on the 22nd July.

Later, after the creation of the Special Constabulary, a Protestant state militia, the *"Specials"* would on occasion deliberately open fire during curfew hours with the purpose of causing a reaction from British soldiers, who would then direct gunfire into the Catholic streets which were tightly bound with small kitchen terrace houses. There was also the danger of gas pipes being punctured which could cause lung poisoning.

Before the turmoil of July 1920, in March of that year, the I.R.A. Brigade staff, decided to create a 2nd Battalion within Belfast with Companies in Ballymacarrett, the Market and Carrick Hill. The task was given to Tom Fitzpatrick and Manus O Boyle was asked to take command in Ballymacarrett.

Both men were officers in the 1st Battalion and Manus O Boyle worked locally as a cashier in the Chemical Works

Manus O Boyle set about recruiting local men and he was helped in this task by a local former British soldier, John –[Sean] Cunningham, from Comber Street.

John Cunningham became the Company 2/I/C.

Manus O Boyle later recorded the following:

"I know that the heaviest fighting took place in the Ballymacarrett area, where there were about 7,000 Catholics.

On the outskirts of that area were about 40,000 Orange men and women.

St. Matthews's church, Convent and Schools were the continuous target of the Orange hordes.

In the early days, it was chiefly a stone-throwing competition, until the Volunteers got organised.

I was detailed then by the Brigade to organise a Company of Volunteers for the defence of Ballymacarrett.

I succeeded in forming a Company of about 120 men.

These were all unemployed. Then the fighting proper commenced as we were now armed with small arms and grenades.

It was a continuous street fight in Ballymacarrett.

Our opponents were heavily armed and had the assistance of the Police and Military.

This continued all through 1920 and up to the Truce.

The nuns were magnificent, Mother Teresa, Sister Eithne, Sister Peter Paul and Sister Bridget are four that I remember particularly....

Mother Teresa could always present us with hundreds of rounds of .45 ammunition that she received from...... [Inspector Mc Connell] , a Catholic R.I.C. officer."

Tom Fitzpatrick recorded one of the earliest actions taken by the 2nd Battalion against Crown Forces:

"Some time about February or March 1920, after the military had taken over a place in the Low Market, where they kept a lot of vehicles, we threw a few bombs into it.

That was a Battalion job and it was done very quietly.

There was no sanction from the Brigade for it.

At that time, the Brigade were averse to activities in Belfast for fear of reprisals on the Catholic population."

Tom Fitzpatrick, a native of County Cavan and WW1 veteran taken at an I.R.A. training camp at Glenariff, August 1921.

CROSS AND PASSION CONVENT BRYSON STREET

On Wednesday 19th September 1900, the new Convent at 2, Bryson Street officially opened when the first two sisters of the Order arrived in Ballymacarrett from England.

At the end of the following month, October 1900, the Convent was formally blessed and within the year, nine Sisters were in residence.

St. Matthews Girls School in near-by Lowry Street became integrated with the Order and was recognised as a Convent National school in November 1901. Thus began an association that would continue for the next 84 years until 1985. The school had over 400 pupils on its role and the sisters began teaching there from 4th November 1901.

The Convent and St. Matthew's Church were located on the dividing line at the top end of Bryson Street between Nationalist Ballymacarrett and Unionist East Belfast.

When the conflict broke out in Belfast on the 21st July 1920 with the expulsion of Catholic workmen from the Shipyard, the church and convent came under attack for the first time and was now at the centre of escalating street warfare.

The following our extracts from a Diary kept by one of the sisters; Sister Veronique O' Riordan and give a unique first-hand account of the period.

1920 - July 21st:

"Today the Catholics were cruelly beaten in the Shipyard; old men were thrown into the Lough. Workmen had to run from the yard chased by thousands of Orangemen, who were joined by a drunken mob at the foot of Frazer Street opposite St. Matthews Church".

"Then commenced the organized campaign of destruction and murder on the Catholics, shops were looted and homes burned.

Many left homeless and penniless in a few hours.

The mob marched into Bryson Street and attacked the Church and Convent.

July 23rd:

"The riots still continue, on Friday morning the Mother Superior and four sisters of the community were advised to leave the Convent [orders from Police].

A machine gun was fitted on a front window facing Bryson Street.

[The Sisters moved for a few weeks to the Good Shepherd Convent on the Ormeau Road and then to the Cross and Passion Convent at Ballycastle. For a short period, the British Army occupied the Convent placing a machine gun post in the Mother Provincial's room which overlooked Bryson Street.

The nuns returned to the Convent on 21st August, less than four weeks later.]

August 21st:

"Sisters returned to the Convent, it was a sad home-coming, the military had left earlier in the week and had left the Convent a wreck.

Not a pane of glass in any window, the front door was boarded up, nothing but destruction all over.

A number of young men from the parish took turns in guarding the Church and Convent night and day."

August 26th:

"At 4pm another attack was made on the Church and Convent. A mob of some thousands arrived equipped with revolvers and petrol tins to finish the work they began on July 22nd, but our Catholic boys numbering only 30 drove the attackers away in about 10 minutes. The mob ran down their own streets and were out of sight when the military arrived."

[This is the first recorded reference to any action carried out by the local I.R.A. Company, or Defence Pickets during the conflict period.]

[Mass was said again in the Convent on 4th September and it re-opened on the 25th September.]

September 18th:

"Yesterday was a day of continuous rioting, the poor people of the parish are suffering terribly, but are most patient".

October 21st:

"Children sent home from school for safety as riots broke out again, they will not be able to return for some days"

1921:

May 29th:

"Owing to the disturbed state of the district all the schools had to be closed this week.

The Catholics have suffered terribly during the past few days. A number of them had to go into the Orange locality to record their votes for the election of members to the new Northern Parliament.

Many of them were badly beaten; others were stabbed with knife blades.

Seaforde Street was attacked by an Orange mob from three sides, but thank God the Catholic boys were able for them. Schools reopened."

Billy Murray of Chemical Street who joined the Volunteers in Greenock while working in Scotland in 1914, recalled those early weeks of August 1920 :

"For about the first three weeks of the riots it was a pitiful sight to stand in Seaforde Street and see families coming in from all the outside areas looking for some place to shelter. When Catholic families fled, the mob went into the house, took everything out and piled it in the street and set fire to it".

"Manus O'Boyle regulated a small number of volunteers [around the Convent area] and a few men who volunteered to help. They were split into two sections for pickets at different times during the night and for different nights during the week.

All these men were armed. James Faloona, Sean Cunningham and myself stood picket duty every night for three weeks without relief. We were armed and had plenty of small arms ammunition.

When the new picketing regulations came into operation, it was much better.

The district was divided into four section areas, each Section Commandant mobilised and regulated his own pickets. All arms and collections; everything pertaining toward control and discipline in the district was under the authority of the IRA".

THE SWANZY KILLING

A Detailed Account on how the I.R.A. Executed the R.I.C. Assassination Squad Responsible for the Murder of Cork City's Sinn Fein Lord Mayor, Tomás MacCurtáin in 1920

The Coroner's Jury into the murder of Tomás MacCurtáin in Cork had found that the *'murder was organized and carried out by the Royal Irish Constabulary officially directed by the British Government.'* District Inspector Oswald Swanzy and the R.I.C. Commissioner G.F. S. Smyth, a former British Army Colonel and a native of Banbridge, Co. Down, were found to be directly indicted in the murder. Smyth was swiftly shot dead by three I.R.A. volunteers (led by Dan *'Sandow'* Donovan) as he visited the Cork Country Club on the 17th of July 1920.

Loyalist violence erupted in Banbridge following Smyth's killing. Catholic houses and business premises were attacked, burned and wrecked by rampaging mobs. The sectarian attacks which had been brought to boiling point by a continued stream of vehement anti-Catholic comments and reports in the Unionist press spread to Dromore, Lisburn and Newtownards.

Smyth's body was brought north for burial in Banbridge, and on the day of his funeral, 21st July, the spark that lit the fires in Belfast was ignited. This was the excuse used **'to activate the pogrom'** against Catholics.

A violent onslaught was made upon the Catholic employees in the Belfast Shipyard. Serious sectarian rioting and sniping began, Catholic public houses were looted, and homes and business premises attacked and burned, resulting in nineteen people killed in the opening week as the war reached Belfast. Protestant mobs and snipers defied a weak and indulgent police while the British Army indiscriminately swept the streets with gunfire in order to clear them. They would at times remain indifferent, as I.R.A. snipers did what they could in order to repel mob onslaughts. The scene was set and the cast dyed as Belfast was engulfed in daily shooting.

Following Smyth's killing, the British decided to move Swanzy up north where they thought he would be safe. However, the I.R.A. in Cork City was determined to avenge Tomás MacCurtáin, as was the overall Director of Intelligence, Michael Collins. Swanzy's first northern posting was to Downpatrick but the I.R.A. quickly moved on locating him, and orders were issued to Northern Divisional H.Q., who in turn sent word to Downpatrick to have him shot. A member of the I.R.A. in the town had daily access to the R.I.C. Barracks, so they were able to collate accurate information as to Swanzy's movements.

Here the story takes a strange twist. Apparently feelings were bitter over the decision to reduce a local I.R.A. volunteer in rank, and men within the local company refused to do the shooting unless his rank was restored. (This arose over an earlier incident involving an attack on Crossgar Barracks.)

It was established by Intelligence that Swanzy was to leave the barracks at a certain time one night. An armed I.R.A. member was positioned in a doorway halfway down Irish Street to carry out the shooting. It was a windy night and the gas lamps on the street were extinguished leaving the area in poor light. When Swanzy eventually came out there were three others with him, all with their collars up and heads down to shield themselves from the wind. Unable to identify which was Swanzy, the I.R.A. man decided to shoot nobody, a decision, which apparently enraged Collins when he heard of it. The news would not have been well received by any measure in Cork City. The I.R.A. there took a decision to send men up north and shoot Swanzy themselves. But Collins and the Dublin G.H.Q. were also determined that the job be done and the 1st (Belfast) Brigade were ordered to begin planning the operation.

The man who would oversee it was Rodger McCorley - a young Brigade Officer from the Clonard area of Belfast. In the meantime, Swanzy had been moved to what was considered a safer town - Lisburn. Several men from Cork did travel up to Belfast to liaise with their Belfast counterparts and study the possibility of hitting Swanzy in the Protestant town.

They would have found life in the northeast of the country in stark contrast to their native Cork. The population was not united, and it was much more difficult to operate. Sectarian killings and rioting were rampant in Belfast and the British Forces were making life uncomfortable for active Republicans, as the Unionists engaged in 'their holy war' against Nationalism.

Cork accents in Belfast with British Forces active across the city in large numbers would put not only the men at risk, but also the operation itself. It was however decided at the beginning of August 1920 to make an attempt to shoot Swanzy without proper organized preplanning. In an ironic twist of fate the car carrying the men to Lisburn broke down, and the plan was cancelled. A second attempt was planned this time with pre-planned organization.

Rodger McCorley travelled to Lisburn on Thursday 18th August, and remained there following Swanzy around, building up some intelligence on his movements, and, as McCorley stated himself, more importantly *to identify the man and to ensure the target was Swanzy*. This done, he returned to Belfast, and on Sunday morning he joined a four man execution party consisting of two Cork men; one by the name of Murphy and the other Sam Culhane, the Intelligence Officer for the 1st (Cork City) Brigade who had carried MacCurtáin's own revolver to Belfast especially to shoot Swanzy, Tom Fox of the

Belfast Brigade (later to become a Colonel in the pro-treaty Free State Army, as was McCorley himself) and the driver, Seán Leonard, originally from Tobercurry, Co. Sligo, who was working in Belfast as a taxi driver.

In total, five men including McCorley, travelled to Lisburn on the morning of Sunday 22nd August 1920. They had decided to shoot Swanzy as he went to church, and it was also agreed that Culhane would fire the first shot from MacCurtáin's revolver.

Seán Leonard was to stay in the car which contained rifles and hand grenades as a back-up should they need to fight it out with pursuing R.I.C. men.

As the four men approached Swanzy, McCorley accounts how strange it was that morning that there were not more people than usual around the streets. But this was nothing more than coincidence, perhaps even a sense of edginess or a more acute alertness as to the surroundings. Once identified by McCorley, Culhane opened fire first, before the other three proceeded to shoot. Swanzy fell dead, and the men retreated to the car, now pursued by a gathering crowd. One old retired ex-British Officer tried to hit McCorley with a blackthorn stick, but with '*a flukshot*,' McCorley dislodged it from the old man's hand. By this time, Rodger McCorley found himself way behind the others, and the car had moved some 20 yards before Tom Fox noticed him missing. It came to a sudden halt as McCorley bundled in, and they began in haste for Belfast. As for the R.I.C. the only car they could find to begin any immediate pursuit was outside the town hall. It had gone a short distance when one of its wheels fell off!

At that time communications did not allow for any form of quick reaction, but the R.I.C. and British military would before the day's end; begin a search for the I.R.A. unit. They had stopped outside the city, sending Seán Leonard on his way with a cover story.

But, with the British Forces already checking all taxi movements within the city that morning Seán was later arrested. He was tried and sentenced to death, but a good defense case was instrumented by Tim Healy and the sentence was commuted to 12 years. The two Cork men returned south satisfied that their comrade had been avenged.

Collins' message was that there would be no safe haven anywhere in Ireland, even the Unionist controlled counties of the northeast. At the same time, it was the ordinary

Catholics who were paying the price of I.R.A. success as the pogroms reached a frightening level. As in Banbridge, Catholic families were forced to flee their homes and Catholic owned property burned in Lisburn in an organized campaign. However, it would be on the streets of Belfast that street- warfare would be unleashed as a better armed and more organized I.R.A. found itself not only having to defend Nationalist areas, but also to engage in offensive actions against Crown forces. The next two years were set to have a bloody outcome.

Memorial Plaque in Lisburn Cathedral to D.I Swanzy

R.I.C. MURDER SQUADS AND I.R.A. RETALIATIONS IN BELFAST

In August 1920, a clergyman outside of Belfast-[Antrim] handed over 60 Martini rifles to the I.R.A. in the city, thinking they were going to the Hibernians. He was keen that they be used to defend Nationalist districts, but he stated that under no circumstances that the guns be given to the I.R.A. Unknown to him, the men who picked the rifles up, were in fact from the I.R.A.

Rodger Mc Corley stated that the rifles were distributed throughout the various Company areas in Belfast. They used the Mk. 6 .303 bullet, which Mc Corley said the I.R.A. had plenty of, having obtained them from a U.V.F. source. The role being undertaken by the I.R.A. during this period was mainly defensive around convents, schools and churches.

But on Saturday evening, 25th September 1920, the I.R.A. opened fire on two R.I.C. men at Broadway, killing one, who was ironically a Catholic named Thomas Leonard based at Roden Street Barrack. The shooting was a result of a failed attempt to disarm them.

The killing of Constable Leonard sparked the Belfast R.I.C. murder squad [known as the *Cromwell Club*] into action.

Within the next three years, up to three of these squads would operate throughout the city, leaving behind them a trail of carnage and murder.

County Inspector Richard Harrison, a native of Kilkenny, controlled the squads, with **District Inspector John Nixon** as his No.2.

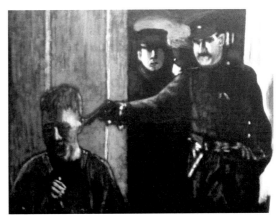

Nixon was posted to Belfast in November 1920, to take charge of C Division, R.I.C. based at Brown Square Barrack, Peter's Hill.

Nixon had already earned himself a reputation during various postings in the south and upon his arrival in Belfast; he began to organize the murder of Catholics.

The following evening after the killing of Constable Leonard, Harrison and his men struck back.

In the early hours of Sunday 26th September 1920, four men with covered faces and carrying rifles, broke into the home of Eamon Trodden and shot him dead.

Eamon "*Ned*" Trodden had been a member of the IRB and at the inception of the Volunteers; he joined the movement, remaining loyal to the Irish Volunteers after the split in September 1914.

His home at 68 Falls Road was a regular meeting place for local IRB members and he also held the position of secretary of the Sean McDiarmada Sinn Fein Cumaan.

He stood in the elections of January 1920 and his proposer was Dan Turley Director of Elections and a volunteer from Dunmore Street in the Clonard district.

On the same night, two others died at the hands of the murder gang Sean Mc Fadden and Sean Gaynor were also murdered in their homes on the Springfield Road. As in the case of the Trodden killing, armed men arrived at the Gaynor home at 236 Springfield Road in the guise of a raiding party.

The Gaynor home was very close to the barrack and both sons of the household were republicans. Liam, a schoolteacher and member of the IRB, joined the Volunteers pre-1916 and Sean was an original member of B Coy, 1st Battalion, which he joined at its inception.

Liam was not in the house that night as he was in Dublin, but Sean was shot, first in the chest and then in the head. James Gaynor, their Father had been a regular soldier serving in the Royal Irish Regiment. He re-enlisted during WW1, serving in the Royal Irish Fusiliers, until his discharge in August 1918.

Along the same road at No. 54 Springfield Road, Sean Mc Fadden was cut down by revolver fire.

Thousands turned out for the funerals.

Ned Trodden was buried in Milltown Cemetery the following Tuesday 28th September, while the Belfast Brigade led by their O/C Joe McKelvey and Sean O Neill, marched behind the hearse at the funeral of Sean Gaynor.

Sean Mc Fadden, a blacksmith by trade, was a Trade Union man and not a member of the I.R.A.

With the help of some sympathetic Catholic members of the R.I.C.-[One of whom was an I.R.A. Intelligence officer], along with a highly placed I.R.A. agent, I.R.A. Intelligence was able to build an extremely detailed file on members of the Murder Gangs, on whom Michael Collins as Director of Intelligence took a direct interest.

The file contains information on all the murders carried out by the R.I.C. in Belfast.

In relation to the Springfield Road murders, it tells us:

> *"At midnight, a party of R.I.C., under County Inspector Harrison, left Springfield Road Barrack, separated into three bands and preceded in shooting up the Falls and Kashmir districts, afterwards entering the houses of the following men who were shot dead.*
>
> *Edward Trodden, who was in his bed when the party under Harrison entered, was pulled out of his bed and dragged by the hair downstairs and shot in the yard.*
>
> *The party then proceeded to the Springfield Road, entered the house of Sean Mc Fadden who met the party in the passage and was shot in three places.*
>
> *A second party led by Constable Giff, forced an entrance into Gaynor's house and shot him in the bedroom. Giff, before leaving the room drove a bayonet through Gaynor's body, fired shots through the rooms in the house and threatened Gaynor's mother with the butt of his rifle, for refusing to disclose the whereabouts of her elder son, Liam.*
>
> *The members of this gang were:*
>
> *Harrison, who shot Trodden and Mc Fadden; Giff, who shot Gaynor, Sergeant*
>
> *C.Clarke [killed in March 1922]; Sergeant Glover [killed in July 1921]; Sergeant Hicks of College Square Barracks and Constables Golding, Cladwell, Sterritt, Gordon, Cooke, Packenham and Norton."*

Head Constable Giff was particularly brutal in his method of killing and tried to ensure his victims died a painful death. One of the ways in which he done this was by using his bayonet before shooting them, as he considered it prolonged their agony.

Giff was also alleged to be involved in the murder of 22 year old Malcahy Halfpenny of 21 Herbert Street, murdered on the 12th June 1921.

The Trodden and Gaynor murders led to grave discontentment amid the rank and file of the I.R.A.'s 1st Battalion as the Brigade Staff at the time would not sanction enthusiastic reprisals.

They preferred to strengthen defence plans for Nationalist areas, which was very much a method of *trial and error.*

Rodger Mc Corley recalled that at a 1st Battalion Council meeting later in the year, **younger members, especially from B and C Companies, forced the issue again, of carrying out executions of known members of the murder gangs.**

As a new and much bloodier year of 1921 dawned in Belfast, Mc Corley would get his way and the I.R.A. would begin to strike back.

Following the events of July 1920, the I.R.A. in Ballymacarrett began to organize the Company for armed defensive measures against Loyalist attacks.

On the 25th October, 1920, black flags were erected in Nationalist districts following the death on hunger strike of the Lord Mayor of Cork Terrance Mc Sweeny.

Flags were erected around the Short Strand, including the bottom of Khartoum Street attached to a post on the railway bank.

At around 1.30pm Loyalist mobs rushed toward the lower end of Foundry Street from both the railway yard and Middlepath Street, but they got no further than the railway arch, as to quote the *Irish News*, "**Defenders rushed to the rescue of the inhabitants of the locality.**"

The attacking mob was beaten back across the railway bank and the lower end of Foundry Street was quickly cleared.

Revolver shots rang out during the melee, during which a [Protestant] man, Joseph McLeod aged 25 of 45 Church Street East was shot in the head and died.

The I.R.A. had opened fire during the rioting that ensued to disperse the Loyalist mob.

Following the shooting, raids were conducted and Henry Megraw, aged 20 was arrested in Young's Row. He was charged with the shooting, but later acquitted. Henry Megraw appears on B Company's nominal role.

In the latter months of 1920, the British Government showed no sign of modifying its Irish policy and the Partition Bill went ahead without any notable concession.

The creation on an official level of the **Ulster Special Constabulary** was as James Craig [Carson's Lieutenant and now Parliamentary Secretary to the Admiralty] said;

"A solution to the mounting unrest in the province and in particular the spread of rebel influences."

The creation of such a force aroused bitter resentment amongst the Nationalist population. Joseph Devlin epitomized his fear *"that the Specials would be used to exterminate the Catholics of Belfast."*

Such was the fear of what could only be referred to as a State militia created solely to implement Unionist policy.

On the 20th November, 1920 the Newry *Frontier Sentinel* said: *"These Special Constables will be nothing less than the dregs of the Orange Lodges, armed and equipped to overawe Nationalists and Catholics."*

Hammer Greenwood, Britain's Chief Secretary to Ireland, answered Devlin's cry in the British House of Commons on the 22nd October, that the creation of the Specials was an *"organized conspiracy to place the lives and liberties of the Catholic minority at the mercy of opponents, armed by the British Government."* by saying that the new force contained *"well-disposed citizens who could be used to assist the police in the preservation of the peace."*

By the 11th November, Greenwood would inform the House that 2,000 applications had been received, but refused to answer Devlin's query as to how many Specials were former U.V.F. men.

Andrew Bonar Law, leader of the Conservative/Unionist Party, a ruthless political partisan of Protestant Ulster stock, referred to the Specials as being; *"selected solely because of their reliability in dealing with a specially difficult situation".*

B Special Mobile Patrol

This strength of the Unionist state was increased by the presence of 16 Battalions of British troops, which it was planned to replace upon withdrawal by the C Specials , establishing a Loyalist state controlled by a Northern Ireland government.

These C Specials were armed, trained and formed into Brigades which were called Groups, of which there were three; the First and Second Group being in Belfast.

It was estimated that the Specials had cost the British government, £1,500,000 in 1921-1922, rising to £2,700,000 for the period of 1922-1923.

C Specials pose outside Murrays Public House on the Mountpottinger / Albertbridge Rd corner April 1922

PARTITION AND STREET WARFARE IN BELFAST 1921

The new year of 1921 was marked by an escalation of the military conflict between the British forces and the I.R.A., whilst the British Cabinet oscillated between a policy of coercion and one of conciliation.

Michael Collins in his position as Minister for Finance pushed De Valera to work toward a policy on the north.

"The north-east must not be allowed to settle down in the feeling that it is a thing apart from the Irish nation", he impressed on De Valera.

He believed an effort be made to work with Republican/Nationalist controlled councils, such as in Tyrone and Fermanagh. By bringing them under the Dail, it would be possible to reduce the partitioned counties to four.

This policy could be broadened to Derry Corporation and other numerous small bodies and to certain fairly large districts within counties- **by internal fragmentation, render the state non-viable.**

De Valera took Collin's viewpoint on board and then pursued to create a pact with the Nationalist Party. The pact was endorsed by the Bishop of Down and Connor, Dr.Mac Rory.

With elections looming in the north and plans to have the Northern Ireland parliament functioning by June, secret talks began to form a working agreement between the two Nationalist parties.

This was finalised at the end of March 1921 and was co-ordinated by one of the Sinn Fein leadership in Belfast, Sean Mc Entee, who represented South Monaghan in the Dail. The pact was endorsed by an 800 strong Nationalist conference in Belfast on the 4th April, chaired by Joseph Devlin, **Canon Crolly, PP St. Matthews,** Ballymacarrett and Downpatrick solicitor, Michael Johnston, entered the pact motion.

.

The meeting called for the establishment of an all-Ireland constituent assembly.

For the first time, in recent years, there now existed some form of official Nationalist voice acting in unison.

The Nationalist campaign for the elections was handicapped by a lack of funds and manpower. Sinn Fein's campaign organizer, Eamon Donnelly from Middletown, County Armagh and a number of their nine candidates were on the British *"Wanted List".*

When the elections did come at the end of May 1921, the Unionists in the north had a sweeping victory cementing their claim for a separate parliament.

The Nationalists secured 12 seats, with Sinn Fein winning the majority of the vote-[104,716] although the seats were split evenly.

Widespread intimidation of Catholic voters was orchestrated by the Specials-the *Irish News* reported that, particularly in East and West Belfast, "**thousands of Catholic voters were forcibly and brutally prevented from exercising their franchise**"

In the south, 120 Sinn Fein candidates were returned unopposed, simply creating a second Dail.

Within the 1RA, there was growing pressure to begin striking back at the R.I.C. and at the end of January 1921, two members of the R.I.C. were shot in the Railway View Hotel-[Roddys], Oxford Street, close to Musgrave Street Barrack.

This shooting was carried out as a direct result from GHQ in Dublin.

A former I.R.A. volunteer named Gilmartin had been brought north for safe keeping as he was prepared to give evidence against a former comrade who had been arrested in connection with the killing of an R.I.C. Inspector in Thurles. GHQ ordered his execution.

The I.R.A. obtained intelligence from a barman who worked in the hotel and was a volunteer in C Company, 1st Battalion, as to the room being occupied by the R.I.C. men and the intended target, Gilmartin.

A four man unit struck on the night of 26TH January, 1921. Forcing entry into the room, they opened fire, killing one Constable immediately and seriously wounding a second. The unfortunate Gilmartin was also seriously wounded.

The second Constable, died shortly afterwards.

Once again, as with Inspector Swanzy, Michael Collins was sending out a clear message that the northeast was not a safe haven for British personal.

Following this shooting, a special I.R.A. "Squad" was established in Belfast. The unit was based in Danny Mc Devitt's tailor's rooms on the 1st floor, 5 Rosemary Street, in the city centre. The Squad would hit at what Rodger Mc Corley described as "*targets of opportunity*".

In March, the Squad struck again, shooting an R.I.C. man on the 4th of the month and a week later, 11th March, two Auxiliaries were shot dead in Victoria Street. Three civilians were also wounded, one of whom a Protestant man from Austin Street, Ballymacarrett, died later in hospital.

The military carried out raids in Nationalist districts the following day and minor skirmishes were reported in the Short Strand.

The three Auxiliaries-[Black and Tans] were based at Gormanstown in County Meath and were in Belfast to collect and drive military vehicles back to their depot.

The R.I.C. member shot on the 4th of the month, died three days after this shooting.

The following month, on the 22nd April, the Squad again picked their targets in the city centre close to their base. Two Auxiliaries were shot and two civilians wounded in an exchange of fire at the junction of Donegal Place and Fountain Lane.

The two wounded Auxiliaries who died were:

John Bales and Earnest Bolam. Both men were WW1 veterans.

John Bales had served in the Norfolk Yeomanry and later the Royal Flying Corp.

Earnest Bolam had saw service with the Kings Liverpool Regiment.

Following the killings of the two R.I.C. Auxiliaries, the R.I.C. "Murder Squad" hit back again in the west of the city. The victims were two brothers, Patrick and Daniel Duffin, both republicans, who lived at 64 Clonard Gardens.

The R.I.C. personnel involved were:

Sergeant's Hicks and Clarke along with Constables Caldwell and Golding from Springfield Road Barrack.

While it could be argued that Harrison's Squad targeted Republicans, in what was purely a policy of *"fighting fire, with fire"*, the same cannot be said of the Nixon Squad, who murdered innocent Catholics.

Roger McCorley

Within two weeks of the Duffin killings, District Inspector, Ferris of Springfield Road Barrack was just leaving St.Pauls Presbytery in Cavendish Street, when he was cut down by a volley of revolver shots fired by three I.R.A. volunteers.

Ferris was one of several men Rodger Mc Corley had marked for execution due to their links with the R.I.C. murder squads.

Ferris survived the shooting but was seriously wounded.

Not so fortunate was Sergeant Glover who was implicated in the Gaynor/Trodden killings. He was shot and killed on the 10th June and two others with him; Constables Sullivan and Sharkey, wounded as they patrolled along Cupar Street. Sergeant Glover had served in the Irish Guards during World War 1; one of seven brothers all of whom saw service including two in the US army. He was discharged after being wounded for a second time in 1917 and re-joined the RIC in 1919.

Constable Sharkey survived his wounds, later joining the RUC. He retired in 1943 with his final posting being Mountpottinger Barracks.

Following the shooting, indiscriminate firing by the Auxiliaries in trucks took place in the Falls Road district just before curfew.

Within the little kitchen houses at curfew hour, lamps were turned down so low as to give the barest of light. Black shawls which women draped around their shoulders by day, were hung across windows to prevent any glimmer of light showing through into the street. Fires would be dampened down so that prowling R.I.C. cage cars could see no smoke.

Meantime, the defence procedure in place for Nationalist districts was being changed to what Mc Corley described as *"an elastic system"*, moving men around from point to point, forming a new firing position as soon as one was lost.

Another idea developed was to break holes in the interlinking walls of the terrace backyards to enable men to pass down streets without being observed or shot at by military patrols.

Rodger Mc Corley states the system of the holes was created due to the fact that they were losing men, captured climbing over yard walls.

In some previous accounts written on this period, it was wrongly stated that the system of the backyard holes was to protect civilians from sniper fire. They certainly used them, but it was designed primarily for use by the I.R.A.

[*I first write about their use by the I.R.A., in a magazine called "The Troubles"-issue 1, in 2001.-author.*]

Another improvement followed in June, with the simple idea of using multi-coloured torches, which the I.R.A. managed to get their hands on.

Pickets were based at a main entrance to a district in view of each other. A *white* signal indicated a sighting of R.I.C./Military patrols.

If the patrols passed by, a *green* signal was flashed, but if they entered into the area, a *red* light was signalled.

Another picket armed with rifles would be positioned behind the Signal picket and they would then engage the patrols.

Shooting intensified in Nationalist districts through the months of May and June.

On the 17th May, R.I.C. patrols were attacked with gunfire and Mills bombs on the Springfield Road, while two days later; several people were shot and wounded in Ballymacarrett.

Four people were shot and wounded in Seaforde Street following an "anti-partitionist" meeting, including a thirteen year old girl.

As the meeting dispersed at Lowry Street, Loyalist gunmen fired down Seaforde Street. A mob then attempted to surge down the street, but was forced back.

The I.R.A. opened fire in response to the shooting directed from the Newtownards Road.

The defensive fire from Seaforde Street caused the Specials to begin firing down the street from Crossley tenders, during which two of those shot were wounded.

In a two day period-[12th-14th] of June, gun-battles occurred in the Clonard district and also in the Docks area, during which a B Special-[Thomas Sturdy of Court Street Barrack] was shot and killed sitting in his Crossley tender. The Specials retaliated by killing two innocent Catholics in their homes in Dock Street.

The month of July was ushered in with two R.I.C. men shot and killed in Union Street on the 6th of the month. Two days later, R.I.C., Specials and British troops mounted a raid into Carrick Hill and a prolonged gun battle began between the I.R.A. and the raiding parties, lasting for over an hour.

A similar raid two days later in the Pound Loney area of the Falls Road, resulted in the death of an R.I.C. man, Thomas Conlon and the wounding of a Special. A Crossley tender was also badly damaged by a "*mine-type* "bomb.

People gather at Royal Avenue / North Street Junction as shooting is in progress in the Carrick Hill area.
Belfast Evening Telegraph

FOOTNOTE

ASU MEMBERS:

SEAMUS WOODS
RODGER Mc CORLEY
SEAMUS Mc KENNA
SEAMUS HERON
JOSEPH MURRAY
SEAN KEENAN
THOMAS FOX
J.FINN

The ASU or the "Squad" based themselves within the city centre at Danny Mc Devitt's Tailor's Room on the first floor of 5, Rosemary Street. Danny was a member of the Republican Movement as was his wife who was a member of Cumann na mBhan.

The *Roddy's* shooting was carried out by :

SEAMUS WOODS
RODGER Mc CORLEY
SEAMUS Mc KENNA
JOSEPH MURRAY

The shooting of the two Auxcilliers on Friday 11th March, 1921 was carried out by:

SEAMUS WOODS
SEAMUS Mc KENNA
SEAN KEENAN
SEAMUS HERON

The Auxiliaries had been reported to be drinking in the *Rose and Crown* public House in Arthur Square, but when the IRA arrived they had just left and were then trailed walking toward Victoria Square. Here they attracted the company of two girls. The IRA men knew that they had to act before the Auxiliaries entered Victoria Street and despite having concern for the girls, they made no hesitation in their decision to strike. Walking four abreast, they drew their revolvers just as the group; two Auxiliaries and the girls passed the Empire Theatre and opened fire. The IRA men then made good their escape leaving the Auxiliaries slumped on the ground along with one of the girls who suffered a slight leg wound.

- The following morning it was reported that a male civilian had also been reported killed during the attack, which baffled Seamus Mc Kenna as the man's body was found outside Johnston's Motor garage some 70 yards beyond the point of the shooting.

- Seamus Mc Kenna concluded in a his statement to the Bureau of Military History made many years later, that the unfortunate man had in fact been shot by one of the Auxiliaries who had in a state of confusion and badly wounded, staggered toward Victoria Street, discharging his weapon.

- He further stated that they would have known this upon investigation of the scene and the spent bullet cartridges but concluded it suited the Unionist press to attribute the killing to the IRA.

The Shooting carried out on Saturday evening, 23rd April, 1921 of two Auxiliaries involved:

SEAMUS WOODS
RODGER Mc CORLEY
SEAMUS Mc KENNA
JOSEPH MURRAY

[*Seamus Woods and Rodger Mc Corley fired the fatal shots*]

The two men were part of a contingent of 21 Auxiliaries who had arrived in Belfast to collect vehicles and drive them back to Gormanstown. They were staying at the Prince of Wales hotel in Victoria Street.

The ASU had been tracking members of the contingent earlier in the day around the City Centre and at one point was going to strike as they went into the GPO in Royal Avenue, but decided against it.

When they did strike, later that evening, they shot two Auxiliaries in Donegal Place, close to Fountain Lane.

Across the island of Ireland during the period of 1920 and 1921, the guerrilla war being waged by the I.R.A. had spearheaded a political drive to settle the conflict. Negotiations were underway between the Republican Leadership and the British government and on Friday July 9th 1921, an order was dispatched to all I.R.A. divisional areas:

"In view of the conversation now being entered into by our government with the government of Great Britain, and in the pursuance of mutual conversations, active operations by our troops will be suspended as from noon on Monday 11th July."

Risteard UaMaolchatha
[Richard Mulcahy]
Chief of Staff.

The truce was signed on Friday 9th July and was to take effect from noon on Monday, 11th July. But while the rest of Ireland celebrated, *Belfast bled.* There was a de-escalation of fighting throughout the 26 counties and the truce was held with effect, but in the northeast, the fighting continued and Belfast was to witness a particularly vicious summer of violence. **The Unionists felt that they were being sacrificed on the high altar of political pragmatism and there was a lack of will on the part of the northern Unionist administration to pursue the opportunity for peace.**

That weekend in Belfast, the truce was ushered in with *"blood letting"* The "Specials" [A part-time uniformed police militia drawn from the Protestant population] backed by Loyalist gunmen, were determined to launch an onslaught on Nationalist districts. The I.R.A. throughout Belfast was mobilized in order to defend their areas, as the Specials and U.V.F. gunmen unleashed sniper fire and moved with armoured cars against the Nationalist areas. The Carrick Hill enclave in the north of the city was near to breaking point and was only one hour short of running out of ammunition when the British military commander in the city organized an implementation of the truce.

Sixteen people died of whom eleven were Catholic and 161 homes were destroyed. Fierce gun-battles, involving machine-gun and rifle fire, as well as handguns and mills bombs were reported along the streets interlinking the Falls and Shankill Roads. Heavy shooting was also reported in the Falls and Cullingtree Road, Millfield and Carrick Hill areas.

Four of the Catholic victims were ex-servicemen. Over the next few days as the Orange marching season reached its climax, shooting occurred around the Short Strand and North Queen Street districts. Two people died and thirty more were wounded on the 14th July, while on the following day as sniping continued in the North Queen Street/York Street area, two R.I.C. policemen were shot and wounded in Little Georges Street. A Unionist politician, William Grant was also wounded by a sniper.

Former B Company volunteer Billy Murray recalled in his personal memories

"Sniping into the Catholic areas became a favourite pastime after working hours.

A large number of Catholic people were wounded and a few killed outright.

The military tried time and again to put an end to this sniping and they were successful in a few areas, even using armoured cars in the attempt.

The IRA succeeded in procuring a number of new rifles including some Lee Enfields. It was easy getting ammunition at this time both from the Police and the Military.

A number of men in B Company went through the war in France and had little to learn about sniping. So these men put a sudden end to most of the Loyalist snipers who were terrorising the Catholic area.

It was rumoured that a truce was being arranged between the IRA and the British and for nights preceding the truce every man in B Company and a host of men from the district remained ready armed with everything from bayonets to Lee Enfield rifles.

On the day before the truce two men arrived back from Belgium and Paris loaded down with small arms such as Peter the Painters, Parabellums, Webleys and a good supply of ammunition to fit.

These were very welcome in this area".

Following the truce of July 1921,

"The IRA established camps up behind Divis Mountain and training started outdoors.

B Company went into camp behind Divis about the end of August for three weeks.

Toward the end of September, a Brigade Officers training camp was opened at

[Name blanked by author] **Farm** [Glenariff] **County Antrim**. **The O.C of B Company was the training officer.**

The training went well for about three weeks. One night a telegram arrived to break camp and come back to Belfast as quick as possible. It was believed that the truce was about to be ended. A disagreement had taken place between the Irish delegates and Lloyd George. Also fighting had broken out all round the Nationalist areas in Belfast. This sniping and bombing was increasing in ferocity every day."

"Owing to irregularities discovered in the Irish White Cross administration in Belfast, the IRA took over complete control.

The ground floor of St.Mary's Hall was likened to the Labour exchange and run on the same system. Money was paid out to the expelled workers three days per week.

Armed guards were to be seen inside the wicker gates leading up to General O'Duffy's offices. All persons going through these gates had to produce a written permit or had to get someone out of the office to identify him.

B Company supplied a guard at these gates for two days a week; A section leader and four men. It was usually my section that did this duty between 9am and 5pm.

I, as section leader always carried the webleys in a small Gladstone bag. I always walked by myself; two men some distance in front and two at a distance behind.

We usually went via the Albert Bridge, up May Street, around the City Hall and along Royal Avenue".

OPEN WARFARE IN BALLYMACARRETT 1921 - 1922

Following the truce, the I.R.A. GHQ in Dublin sent Eoin O Duffy, the I.R.A. commander in Ulster to Belfast to act as a Liaison Officer with the British military in the city. He set up his headquarters in St. Mary's hall in the Smithfield area, but found Belfast not to be on the same level as other cities in the rest of the country.

The British military seemed content to respect the truce in its initial stages, but the Specials who were acting as the armed wing of the northern administration, which had been officially constituted by the British King in June, continued to act against the Nationalist areas with the full endorsement of the Belfast Parliament.

Reference to the period is made in an I.R.A. divisional report sent by Seamus Woods O/C of the 3rd Northern Division, which covered Belfast, to I.R.A. GHQ on the 27th July 1922, when he states;

"Until the signing of the treaty in London, the perfecting of our organization, training and equipping had been pursued with great earnestness on the part of all officers and men. As both Numbers 2 and 3 Brigades were very much below strength in July'21, a large number of recruits were taken on in these areas".

The increase in recruits was due largely to the truce and the fact that as Woods states in the same report: "the *Catholic population believing for the moment that we had been victorious and that the Specials and U.V.F. were beaten, practically all flocked to our standard, with the exception of the aristocratic minority."*

Throughout Ireland, the I.R.A. used the truce for intensive training. It was important to maintain discipline, as grievances on both sides were still sore.

In the same report Seamus Woods made reference to the fact that the truce was not been adhered to and officers and men were being arrested.

He also stated that:

"After the raid on their liaison office, St.Mary's Hall, Belfast, in which the name of practically every officer in the Division was found, all the Divisional and many of the Brigade officers demanded an inquiry into the circumstances of the raid and were asking the Divisional Commandant to resign."

[Joe Mc Kelvey]

The truce appeared to have little effect on the situation in Belfast.

In August 1921, the local R.I.C. Commissioner observed in a confidential report:

"Poverty is still rife in the Nationalist Quarters where so many people are existing on charitable donations received from the Expelled Workers Fund, which continues to receive fairly large subscriptions from various sources, particularly White Cross of America."

Training camps were established within the Divisional area at Hannahstown [Belfast], Seaforde and Castlewellan in County Down and Glenariff and Torr Head, in County Antrim.

The I.R.A. in Belfast reached its peak membership during the months of August and September 1921- [835] and would have preferred to now engage in a war against British Crown forces similar to its counterparts in the south, but unfortunately the I.R.A. in the north-east of the country but more especially in Belfast, found itself having to act as defenders of the Nationalist areas against armed Loyalists engaged in sectarian pogroms and the Unionist controlled armed militia in the guise of Special Police

Only in areas such as South Armagh, Tyrone and Monaghan, was the I.R.A. able to operate with a free hand against the Specials and British military.

The need to defend the Catholic community was vital to the Belfast I.R.A. during the 1920-1922 periods, as they struggled not to lose their ideological role as the Army of the Irish Republic. They were also operating in a hostile environment flooded with British troops, Police and Loyalist Specials who targeted the Catholic community in "acts of reprisals" which stretched from merely shooting into Catholic streets during curfew hours in order to prompt a reaction from the military to the inhabitants, to conducting actual murder.

Added to this was the poor social condition in the Catholic working-class districts which was caused in part by expulsions from employment and also the overcrowding due to relatives and friends being forced out of their homes in Protestant districts.

This was a much harsher environment than the *"fighting ground"* of Roscommon, Mayo, or West Cork. It was for these very reasons that the majority of the Belfast I.R.A. would later remain loyal to the pro-treaty Government GHQ in Dublin, who ensured mainly through Michael Collins that they were financed and armed.

For the Officers of the 1st Belfast Brigade or the 3rd Northern Division overall, it was loyalty to a GHQ that logistically supported them, rather than to a treaty that isolated them from their "natural aspiration of a United Ireland".

Michael Collins stands out as the only Republican leader in the south for whom partition and the plight of the northern nationalists remained a major concern. Yet, it's ironic that his desperate efforts to assist the latter, led him to adopt a confusing blend of "non-recognition", diplomacy and coercion toward the Unionist Government in the north-east.

Collins death in August 1922 during the civil war and the new policy of Cosgrave's Cabinet in recognising the Belfast Unionist Parliament, spelt the end of Republican resistance in the north as a real potential threat for the next 48 years and one that when it did come, would be launched from the very streets of Catholic Ballymacarrett that Loyalists tried so hard to eliminate from East Belfast during the period of 1920-1922. [It is also important to empathise that Collins death preceded the atrocities and executions of Republican volunteers carried out during the civil war by Free State forces which were then under the command of Richard Mulcahy and Sean Mac Mahon.

Added to this, the political divisions in northern nationalism ensured that the Catholic minority in the north was effectively precluded from any say in influencing its own fate at a critical juncture in the historic issue of partition.

Despite the I.R.A. in Belfast being forced into a primary role of defence, it still conducted an offensive policy against Crown forces; on the whole this would mainly have been Specials and R.I.C. personnel. The increase in attacks was due to the establishment of "Active Service Units" [ASU], while others were shot during gun-battles that engulfed Nationalist districts. I.R.A. snipers in areas such as Ballymacarrett/Short Strand also fired at trams carrying shipyard workers, while others were bombed as a retaliation for the huge expulsion of the Catholic workforce.

The whole mood of political uncertainty was the signal for a renewed wave of bloody violence at the end of August 1921, during which 21 people lost their lives over a three day period.

The worst of the fighting was around the Catholic York Street district, which lay within the 2nd Battalion area.

The Loyalist attacks was planned to wipe out the Nationalist streets around York Street and send a message to Britain that no settlement involving the I.R.A. was possible in Ulster.

However, Eoin O Duffy mobilised the I.R.A. to defend the area, which broke the siege.

Seven Protestants were killed and the *Manchester Guardian* reported that the I.R.A. ***"was retaliating in kind and quite as effectively as the Loyalist gunmen."***

To further infuriate the Unionists, Michael Collins made a visit to County Armagh and told a 10,000 strong gathering, which included a large force of the I.R.A., that the Dail would not desert them.

[Unfortunately after his death in August 1922, the Dail not only deserted the Nationalists of the north, but it betrayed the Northern Divisions]

The I.R.A. also had an extensive stock of Mills bombs- [grenades] and a large stock of home-made bombs, which were used against mobs attacking Catholic districts. One example of this was when a large Loyalist crowd firebombed the Sextons house close to St. Matthew's Church on the 22nd November 1921. The densely packed mob assembled in the vicinity gloating over their deed, when a bomb was hurled over into their ranks from Seaforde Street killing two and injuring forty-five others. The *Irish News* described the scene of the injured *"laying in heaps of twos and threes"*.

On the 24th November, a shipyard tram travelling along Corporation Street at 5.45pm was attacked when the I.R.A. threw a bomb from Little Patrick Street. The device, which was hurled through a window of the lower part of the tram, blew a section of the tram apart and killed two of the passengers on board.

That particular day ended with a death toll of 14 killed, ten of which were Catholic.

The following evening, Shipyard trams were again fired on at around 7.30pm in the York Street/ North Queen Street area.

Two days later, on the 26th November, amid nightly gun-battles around York Street, North Queen Street and the Short Strand, another tram was attacked in Royal Avenue killing two of its passengers. The Shankill Road bound Shipyard tram was attacked at 6pm as it passed by the Grand Central hotel in the city centre. The two I.R.A. Volunteers involved in the attack were prominent members; one from the Dock area, the other from Carrick Hill. They escaped along Berry Street into Francis Street and safety.

These attacks usually resulted in retaliation against innocent Catholics; vulnerable targets in a bid to take revenge.

A pattern had developed through the month of September into November 1921 with snipers concentrating their fire into and around Seaforde Street, while mobs attacked St.Matthews church and the *Cross and Passion* convent close by in Bryson Street. Both the church and convent were vulnerable to the tightly bound Protestant Streets opposite. The I.R.A. remained active across the district with its own snipers firing into the Protestant streets and at the Shipyard trams.

An extract from the 2nd Battalion operations report to O/C No.1 Belfast Brigade around this time summarises the situation:

> **"During the month there were constant outbreaks by the hostile population in the Battalion area and obviously organised attempts were made by armed gangs of men to invade the Catholic districts.**
>
> **The hostile element was extremely well equipped and in the Ballymacarrett district appeared openly carrying full bandoliers and service rifles.**
>
> **A determined and long threatened invasion of Seaforde Street, Ballymacarrett was attempted.**
>
> **On the 22n – [September], B Coy. Were obliged to take up firing positions for its defence.**

On Sunday 24th large numbers of armed men were observed at the Newtownards Road and Seaforde Street and the position was so threatening that a Mills bomb had to be thrown by one of our men.

The grenade was very effective and two of the Orange mob were killed and 34 wounded."

The I.R.A. defence of the Seaforde Street area infuriated the northern authorities to the point that on the 21st September 1921, prior to another weekend of attacks, one of the most extensive raids to be seen in Belfast by the Crown forces was carried out by the R.I.C. and British military in the Short Strand. For nine hours, they engaged in searches for weapons. Houses and yards across the district were searched by the R.I.C. as the military were posted on the streets. No weapons were unearthed, but the huge presence of Crown forces prevented access to the area for 24 hours by I.R.A. ASUs to reinforce any defensive measure in place by the local company.

During the week period of the 19th-25th November 1921, 27 people died and 92 were wounded across Belfast.

December 1921 continued much in the same vein with snipers active on a daily basis. But it was the weekend of Friday 17th and Saturday 18th December around the Short Strand that saw the worst shooting in the city since York Street at the end of August when the I.R.A. was mobilised.

There had been the usual sporadic shooting leading up to the Friday and on the Wednesday; a Police lorry was raked by machine-gun fire in Seaforde Street. Then on the Friday evening the Seaforde Street area was attacked with unparalleled vigour by Loyalist gunmen and Specials.

Barricades were now erected at the top of Seaforde Street and Young's Row on the Newtownards Road entrance to the district.

The *Irish News* reported in its columns:

"Driven to desperation by the intensity of the onslaught at so many points, the Catholics to maintain their lives and property were compelled to reply and a regular gun battle was in progress."

In reality, it was the I.R.A. replying with gunfire as the district was coming under attack from every end. B Company was now engaged in the worst period to date of shooting to occur since the outbreak of the conflict.

There was no truce or treaty in effect on the streets of Ballymacarrett as the ritual of the snipers bullets swept the tightly bound streets.

The shooting began at 5am and continued throughout the morning.

A member of the Loyalist Ulster Imperial Guard was shot by the I.R.A. close to Young's Row on the Newtownards Road.

The U.I.G. was an organization made up exclusively of Protestant WW1 veterans.

An elderly Protestant man was also caught in the shooting as he made his way home from his job as a Night Watchman. He was shot in early morning crossfire between B Company and Loyalists in the Seaforde Street/Newtownards Road area.

British troops at Seaforde Street also opened fire during the shooting.

The 71 year old man sadly died in hospital twelve days later on 1st January, 1922.

By the following evening B Company and those supporting non-members, were engaged in returning fire across the district until the attacks were repelled and faded out. Four people died two from each community and once again raids were carried out in the

Short Strand by the military and R.I.C. on the Sunday in a search for weapons. The year ended with the death of 109 People across Belfast

1922 continued much as 1921 had ended, with daily shooting throughout the Catholic districts of Belfast. The killing continued and age proved no barrier to the gunmen who imposed their rule amid the tightly bound back-to-back kitchen houses. February's death toll reached 47, with up to 100 wounded. Worst was to come as the spring and summer months would boil to a bloody climax.

The killing of five-year-old John Devlin on February 16th in Seaforde Street when a Loyalist gunman fired a single shot through the barricade at the Newtownards Road entrance at children playing, caused anger in the district despite such shootings being a part of life in a city torn apart by civil war. The same day, Special Constable Mc Adam based at Mountpottinger barrack was shot and wounded in a B Company attack.

The shooting of Specials was to increase as the I.R.A. across the city stepped up its offensive actions and in particular began targeting Specials who would have been seen in the same manner in Belfast and the north, as the Black and Tans would have been in the south of the country.

Two were shot and wounded on the 4th March, one of whom, Special Constable Henderson was shot by B Company in the Mountpottinger area.

The 12th of March began a week-long series of sniping and bomb attacks in and around the Short Strand during which raids were carried out by the Military and Specials on the 15th in a search for weapons. Their presence did not prevent a murder gang penetrating into Thompson Street in the early hours to throw a bomb into the bedroom of a house killing a woman as she slept in bed. Later that morning, two Protestants were shot and wounded as they entered the Glavin stables at the corner of Thompson Street, while a third was shot and wounded in the Corporation Yard on the Short Strand.

That same weekend on the 19th of March, a B Company sniper shot dead a member of the Loyalist Ulster Protestant Association during a gun-battle around the Seaforde Street area of the district, while four days later on the 23rd of the month, an I.R.A. ASU shot and killed two Specials at the corner of May Street.

This date-[23rd March] is synonymous with the brutal slaughter of the Nationalist Mc Mahon family in north Belfast by the infamous R.I.C. murder-gang led by District Inspector John Nixon operating from Brown Square barrack in the Peter Hill area

.

The following day 24th, another murder atrocity was attempted in Altcar Street within sight of Mountpottinger barrack. Three men, alleged to be Specials, entered a house and proceeded to shoot anyone they found there. Peter Murphy aged 61, was the first to be shot followed by Sarah Mc Shane aged 15, before they turned their guns on three years old Mary McCabe. As they ran from the house they fired at, and wounded Nellie Whelan. It was nothing short of a miracle that all those shot survived the ordeal. As with so many murders of that period, proof of identity or justice was not forthcoming.

A week later on the night of April 2nd 1922 similar style shootings were carried out in succession at three houses in the Carrick Hill district again by the Nixon led R.I.C. gang resulting in a further atrocity during which five people died including a seven-year-old boy. Michael Walshe was shot along with his young sister Brigid aged 2, while lying in bed having just witnessed their Father, Joseph a former soldier, been dragged from the bed and cudgelled to death. Michael's sister survived as did his fourteen-year-old brother Frank who was beaten and shot in the small kitchen. Joseph Walsh's baby son Robert aged 8 months died the following day. This was one of

the worst atrocities of the period. The other victims who died that night were Joseph Mc Crory, aged 40 [15 Stanhope Street], Bernard Mc Kenna [26 Park Street] and William Spallin aged 70 [16 Arnon Street].

The Walshe family lived just two doors from the Spallins in Arnon Street. William Spallin had just buried his wife that day and his murder was witnessed by his twelve years old grandchild who was found gazing in horror at the murdered man.

On the night of the Carrick Hill murders, Volunteer Sean Montgomery, an officer in D Company, 1st Battalion was in the area and later gave the following account:

*"**Outsid**e [the house], **were the R.I.C., so I went out through the window to put our**
revolvers on the spouting of the roof.
Then I heard a boy shouting that his daddy was shot.
I came down the stairs and out we went. We were in an end house.
When we got outside an officer of the Norfolk regiment had the driver of a Police Car
against the wall, and three soldiers with rifles at the ready to fire.
He said to the Special that if he did not tell him [who had killed the Catholics] he would
give the order to fire.
He [the Special] **said he had nothing to do with it, but that D.I. Nixon was in charge and**
the Police had told the army they were going to raid.*

Within a week of the attempted Short Strand massacre in Altcar Street, once again in the Mountpottinger area, two Specials were shot and wounded by B Company, one of whom-Special Constable Hale died. In the west of the city on the 14th March, the I.R.A. also shot and killed R.I.C. Sergeant Christy Clarke on the Falls Road as it was strongly believed he was involved with an R.I.C. murder gang which had operated from Springfield Road barrack in 1920. Clarke, a Catholic, is buried within a short distance from the Mc Mahon family in Belfast's Milltown Cemetery. A year earlier in May 1921, another Catholic R.I.C. member, District Inspector Ferris based at Springfield Road barrack was cut down in a volley of shots fired by three I.R.A. volunteers as he left St. Pauls Presbytery on the Falls Road.

Ferris was one of several men Rodger Mc Corley of the I.R.A.'s Brigade Staff had marked for execution because of their links to the Springfield barrack murder gang. Ferris survived the shooting, but was seriously wounded. Not so fortunate was Sergeant Glover who was implicated in the killing of Republicans Sean Gaynor and Eamon Trodden both of whom were murdered in their homes. Sergeant Glover was shot and killed on the 10th June 1921 as he patrolled in Cupar Street along with Constables Sullivan and Sharkey, both of whom were wounded.

Following the shooting carried out by volunteers of the 1st Battalions D. Company, Auxiliaries carried out indiscriminate shooting around the Falls Road area as they patrolled in trucks prior to curfew hours.

The months of April and May 1922 saw the ferocity of attacks upon the Nationalist areas reach a bloody climax. But while the I.R.A. were stretched to the limit in defending the Short Strand and trying to fight off attacks across the Lagan in the north of the city, they were also called upon throughout May into June to engage in a series of offensive actions which included a *"Burning Campaign"* against Unionist owned business premises.

Supplies of rifles much needed by the Belfast I.R.A. began to arrive from GHQ in Dublin during April, as the 3rd Northern Division found itself at the core of a rapidly changing policy being conducted by the Pro-treaty GHQ, which played out as part of the internal politics being conducted in a bid to avert a total split within the I.R.A. and on which side Divisional loyalties would emerge, should, what appeared inevitable, happened.

THE BLOODY CLIMAX: APRIL/MAY 1922.

To describe the months of April and May of 1922 as the "*bloody climax*" of the two years of conflict, would not be overstating the facts.

In the "*battle worn*" districts of Belfast, the savagery and ferocity of the attacks was stepped up.

The political situation was in stalemate following the breakdown of indirect negotiations that were taking place between Collins and Craig to try and reach an agreement and build cordial relations between the Provisional government and the Six-County state.

The month of April had began with the Arnon Street atrocity in Carrick Hill and at the end of the week a gun battle erupted in Ballymacarrett, not between the IRA and Loyalist gunmen which was the norm, but between the Military and Loyalists.

Shooting began around the lower end of the Woodstock Road concentrating on the Woodstock /Lisbon Street area and this gun battle was the beginning of what was to be a concerted series of attacks by Loyalists against the Short Strand and the Marrowbone in the north of the city.

The first attacks came in the Bone district on Monday 17th April, when a siege was made upon the area with Antigua and Sanderson Streets being burned.

These burnings were the beginning of a bloody week that continued the following day when shooting erupted again around the Short Strand side of the district, with snipers operating from the Woodstock and Albertbridge Road.

The shooting continued into the following day, Tuesday, 18th, when, upon the lifting of the curfew at 6am, heavy gunfire began at the top of the Short Strand with snipers firing down Lisbon Street and Woodstock Street into Thompson Street.

As was now the familiar pattern, Catholic Defenders and the IRA returned fire when and where possible as Crossley and Lancia armoured cars carried RIC and military reinforcements into the district.

The first victim was 15 year old John Scott, a Protestant from Well Street who fell victim to a sniper at the corner of Mountpottinger Road.

After two hours the shooting began to subside and a lull fell over the area. But this was to prove a temporary respite and just after 3pm a fresh attack began when a large Loyalist mob, many armed **and led by Specials**, surged from the Alberbridge Road and managed to penetrate into Altcar Street were they attacked homes at the top end of the street.

Shooting now had resumed with greater intensity and a pitched gun battle ensued around the top of the Short Strand/Madrid Street and Albert Bridge.

At around 5.30pm, 32 year old Rose Dougan from Arran Street and a friend 29 year old Mary Berry, were cut down by Loyalist-[Special] sniper. Rose was shot while holding the hand of one of her daughters, Mary aged 8 who watched her mother die. An added tragedy was that Rose was pregnant when she was shot. * {refer to footnote] [1]

Some 30 minutes following this fatal shooting, Loyalist gunmen entered the shop of Patrick Mc Goldrick in Pim Street and shot him dead.

The following day, Wednesday 19th April, events continued in the same intensity beginning at the lifting of the curfew.

The first victim was James Johnston aged 50, a Protestant from My Lady's Road who was shot by an unknown sniper as he made his way to work at Anderson's Felt Works on the Short Strand were he worked as a Foreman.

Later in the day, while shooting continued on the Short Strand, 16 year old John Walker of 97 Short Strand, was shot in the throat killing him. It is unclear who fired the fatal shot as both the British Army and the Specials were firing in the area at the time. One report stated he was shot by a military patrol, while his Mother's pension claim states he was killed during an attack involving an Orange mob and Specials.

John Walker was a member of the Republican Movement having joined the Fianna in 1919 and was killed in the defence of his community.

In the course of the afternoon casualties mounted on all sides.

A Protestant man, James Greeves, was shot and seriously wounded in his own home by a stray bullet. Two B Specials were shot and wounded in Lisbon Street. Daniel Diamond, aged 25 was shot by a Loyalist sniper and died shortly afterwards in the Mater Hospital. Fourteen year old James Greer, a Protestant was shot around the same time and also died in the Mater two days later on Friday 21st.

The situation in Belfast was so bad that on the Friday evening, the Belfast Protection Society wired the following urgent message regarding the plight of the Nationalist community:

The Right Honourable Winston Churchill and Right Honourable Austin Chamberlain.

"Belfast Catholics being gradually but certainly exterminated by murder, assault and starvation: their homes being burned, streets swept by snipers; life unbearable; military forces inactive. Special police hostile; northern government either culpable or ineffective. Your government saved the Armenians and Bulgarians. Belfast Catholics getting worst treatment; last two days appalling".   Rev. B.Laverty Chairman.

No practical help materialised from the appeal. The campaign continued unabated without hindrance or intervention by either the British government or the subordinate Belfast Parliament.

On the Sunday, 23rd, mother of two, Elizabeth Mc Cube, aged 34, was fatally wounded when a bomb was thrown into the church grounds from the Newtownards Road/Bryson Street Street corner. An RIC Constable, John Moriarty, was also wounded in the blast. He was standing on the Bryson Street side of the entrance and may have been the intended target of the bomber. As people carried both victims into the church, gunfire was directed at them and Constable Moriarty who sustained serious leg injuries was further injured by a bullet.

As Mrs McCabe was anointed, women who had gathered inside the church for mass, began praying at the altar, some fearful of the situation.

Safety was sought through the sacristy door into the church grounds and soldiers provided protection as an ambulance arrived. Elizabeth Mc Cabe died shortly afterwards. * [2]

The incident at St.Matthew's church was mentioned in a letter from Michael Collins to James Craig, Prime Minister of the Belfast Parliament on the 28th April, 1922 as Collins raised the question of the persecution of Catholics by armed mobs unhindered by the military or police. Reference was also made to Constable Moriarty. Collins was hard hitting in his words and his letter was detailed as to events in Belfast. He was of course kept up to date with regular intelligence reports and the daily incident reports kept by the 3rd Northern Division and Catholic Protection Society.

In his letter, Collins was concerned that no charitable action had been taken by the Minister for Home Affairs, Dawson Bates, for a shelter to house Catholics burned out of their homes in North Belfast and who were herded together in a pitiful way- men, women and children in wooden huts on waste ground.

He assured Craig: *"those citizens of Orange proclivities and their property will never be refused ample protection by us."*

Also in the letter he stated:

"I am determined that the awful conditions that have been existing in your area since the devolution of certain powers on you, will not be tolerated in the rest of Ireland, but

if you want quick results in this respect, the best way to get them is to protect the lives and property of the 25% of the population of Belfast which is being gradually exterminated.

Many members of the RIC at present in Belfast are anxiously waiting the termination of their contracts with you in order to enjoy security elsewhere in Ireland and avoid the fate intended for Constable Moriarty and meted out to other Constables under your jurisdiction."

Later in the evening, following the bomb attack at the front of St.Matthews, two gunmen burst into the home of a 68 year old blind man, Robert-[Thomas] Miller who was a Protestant living in Beechfield Street. Mr Miller was sitting in his parlour, when the gunmen shot him. A friend who was also in the house at the time was also shot but miraculously survived.

The month of May 1922 saw an upsurge of shooting, bombing, arson and intimidation which resulted in 75 deaths-[42 Catholics and 33 Protestants]

The IRA in Belfast targeted Unionist business premises throughout the month in a *"Burning Campaign"* in what Seamus Woods described as *"a campaign of destruction of enemy property which hit the authors and promoters of the pogrom".*

FOOTNOTE

[1] In 1997, I spoke to Mary Dougan at that time an elderly woman still living in Ballymacarrett. She accounted to me that my Grandmother who lived at 25 Arran Street had held her mother as she died. She also told me that for many years she had in her possession a part of the bullet casing that had killed her mother. [Author]

[2] A Small led cross marks the spot outside the main doors of St.Matthew's church were Elizabeth Mc Cabe was fatally wounded.

John Walker is commemorated on a window within the church.The following month as the I.R.A. stepped up its attacks, the final intimidation of Catholic families from the Protestant area of York Road in the north of the city commenced on Thursday 18th May when any Catholic families still living in Mountcollyer Street were forced to leave their homes. The following day, Friday the 19th, the small Catholic enclave around Weaver Street on York Road found itself at the mercy of Protestant attackers who armed with revolvers forced 148 families from their homes. The little enclave had suffered in previous shooting and bomb attacks and now a final purge was being made to clear Catholics from the York Road area. Within the following few days' nearly 1,000 penniless refugees reached Glasgow. The let-up in intimidation did not end, as more families would be evicted in the first week of June, 436 families in total.

Several thousand people from across Belfast poured into Dublin and Glasgow, while many others absorbed in some way into the already congested Catholic districts.

The *Manchester Guardian* referred to the evictions:

"These people have committed no offence unless it is an offence to be born a Catholic. Hundreds of families are being continually driven from their homes. In these operations the Specials provide the petrol, firearms and immunity from interruption."

The same day as the purge against the Catholics of York Road-[19th May] the I.R.A. in a desperate act of retaliation entered Garretts Co-Operative in Little Patrick Street off Nelson Street in the Dock area and proceeded to line the workers up against a wall. Only one was a Catholic and he was singled out to be placed against another wall. This man must surely have thought he was about to be shot, but the guns were not turned on him but on his workers as a hail of bullets struck down the unfortunate men resulting in four dying.

The previous day Thursday 18th, the I.R.A. carried out a dramatic early dawn raid on the R.I.C. Headquarters at Musgrave Barracks. The I.R.A. party of 21 volunteers, led by Seamus Woods, comprised of men from the 1st and 2nd Battalions. The intention was to attempt to firstly capture, or destroy the Lancia Armoured Cars housed in the barrack which contained 150 R.I.C. personal.

In the ensuing gunfire an R.I.C. man, John Collins was shot and killed and Special Constable Mc Keown was wounded before the I.R.A. had to withdraw into the 2nd Battalion area.

Later that morning, a large force of British troops, R.I.C. and Specials raided Ballymacarrett/Short Strand.

The searches began at 7am and continued until 8.30am and the Convent and school was included in the raids as a possible haven for the raiding party.

No one was arrested, or weapons located and later that day, fierce exchanges of gunfire took place between B Company, Loyalists and Specials.

A few weeks earlier, on the opening day of the month, a large force of Specials raided Foundry Street, Khartoum Street and Kane's Lane, while the military stood picket on the street corners.

A Mills bomb and a revolver were discovered at the railway bank behind Foundry Street and a man arrested for procession of ammunition]

Ballymacarrett, the Bone and Ardoyne districts came in for an onslaught over the weekend of 20th - 21st May.

Constant sniping occurred around the lower end of the Newtownards Road throughout the afternoon of Saturday 20th, beginning at 3.30pm.

Three hours of cross-divide sniping took place as Loyalist gunmen positioned themselves on the rail bridge running across Bridge End, enabling them to direct fire toward the Short Strand.

The British Army engaged snipers on both sides.

In the Marrowbone and Ardoyne to the north of the city, the residents were subjected to a week of their streets being raked with machinegun and rifle fire for around two hours each night until curfew hours-[10pm-6am] by the Specials.

They would advance from their base in extended order to the fields at the back of Ardoyne and generally around 8.45pm, assume prone firing positions and rake gunfire down into the streets.

As the weekend came to a close on Sunday 21st May, the Market district suffered from a regular attack by Specials on foot and in Cage cars. From the safe distance of the Gas Works and the old Slaughter House, they were observed lying on the streets firing into the houses, as people were forced to lie on the floors avoiding the windows as everybody and everything became a target.

The week beginning Monday 22nd May, will not be remembered or recorded in the annals of the conflict for the daily cross divide sniping around the Short Strand which saw two Protestants killed and two B Specials shot and wounded on the Albert Bridge, but more for an event that occurred earlier that morning and was sending shock waves through the Unionist hierarchy. William Twaddell, a member of the Northern Parliament and an outspoken Loyalist who led the Ulster Imperial Guard, was shot dead by two volunteers in Lower Garfield Street in the city centre, as reprisals by the I.R.A. continued.

The killing of Twaddell prompted the Northern Parliament to introduce Internment without trial.

In Belfast, the death toll for May reached 75, [42 Catholics and 33 Protestants], while the following month, 25 people died, [18 Catholics and 7 Protestants]. Despite the campaign of shooting and intimidation by Loyalists taking its toll on the Nationalist areas, the I.R.A. continued its attacks against the Specials across Belfast and the north.

On the same day, William Twaddell was shot; six Specials were wounded across Belfast in sniping, two of those on the Albert Bridge. Two days later, Wednesday, 24th May, a tram travelling along the Mountpottinger Road carrying Protestant workers was fired on and a Special, Constable Hanna was wounded when a bomb was thrown at a patrol in B Company actions.

Three Protestants were killed and thirteen wounded throughout the city, while five Catholics suffered gunshot wounds. Casualty figures fluctuated up and down each day.

The introduction of Internment saw a large concentration of Military, Police and Specials move against Nationalist districts on Tuesday morning of 23rd May at 4am. They were backed by Armoured Cars and the initial raids within Belfast resulted in 39 men being arrested .

Across the Six Counties, similar raids were taking place.

The following morning, Wednesday 24th May, the men were transported in a convoy of Cage Cars from Chichester Street Police barrack to Belfast Prison.

The prisoners were handcuffed in three's, with six prisoners in each Cage Car with a Special standing in each corner with a rifle at the ready.

Billy Murray recalled in the Cage Car that he was , **the Specials were singing *"Kevin Barry, you're a Bastard" "You are a dirty Fenian Basterd"* and while singing kept looking sideways at us prisoners, keeping their rifles pointed at us, or over the side of the cage.**

Republican Prisoners under escort, en-route from G.N.R. to Belfast Prison.

The following day Thursday 25th May, three young children were wounded in gun and bomb attacks in the Seaforde Street area and two Specials, Constables Murphy and Connor died one in the Market, the other in the Falls Road area. Lizzie Curran, aged 9 and Mary Morrison, aged 12, were shot and wounded by Loyalist snipers around Seaforde Street and another child, Jennie Bell, aged 9, was wounded by a bomb in the same area. The month of May ended with the deaths of two more Specials, one on the 29th of the month and another two days later on the 31st of the month.

The underhand politics being instigated in Dublin; the introduction of Internment, coupled with the poor economic and low moral situation in the Nationalist areas; the outbreak of a civil war in the south of the country over the acceptance of the treaty terms with Britain, all combined to erode the I.R.A. in Belfast as an effective fighting force

The flurry of diplomacy taking place between the governments north and south and with the British, was happening against a background of decreasing violence in Belfast. In the city the month of June 1922, saw a marked fall in the number killed with 25 victims- [18 Catholics, 7 Protestants] with a 100 wounded, compared to the month of May.

However in June, there was as mentioned a marked increase of Catholic families evicted from their homes by Loyalists.

Politics was now driving the agenda. The I.R.A. in Belfast was now in an untenable position and it really was *the beginning of the end.*

In its last phrase of activities in the north, the I.R.A. were largely contained to a campaign of burning, mainly of Unionist owned commercial property in Belfast through the month of June.

The purpose of this "burning of property" was as Seamus Woods explained: ***"to hit the authors and promoters of the pogrom."***

By July 1922, B Company was depleted with a skeleton membership. Volunteers had moved south for integration into the Free State Army, while others had been arrested and Interned.

On the 20th July 1922, Seamus Woods who had been appointed the O/C of the 3rd Northern Division at a Divisional meeting on Sunday 9th April, detailed a report to GHQ as to the situation currently in Belfast.

Despite the I.R.A. no longer being an effective fighting group depleted in manpower, Woods states that the Belfast Brigade still comprises:

- **181 Rifles and 11,600 rounds of ammunition**
- **308 Service revolvers and Autos, plus 7,400 rounds of ammunition**
- **5 Thompson Guns and 1,220 rounds of ammunition.**

ENEMY STRENGTH:

- ....**British Military: 5,500**
- ....**RUC: 2,650**
- ....**Uniformed and Semi-Uniformed**
- ....**Specials: 26,680**
- ....**Total Strength: 34,830**

In the report he states:

"The respect-[from the people], has been won not so much out of sympathy with our National aspirations and our fight for National Freedom, but more on account of the part the Army had played in defending the minority against organised attacks by uniformed and non-uniformed Crown Forces."

Seamus Woods in the same report referred to the shooting of two Specials-[Special Constables McGarrety and Roulston at Millfield by the Executive and the reaction by the Specials. Backed by armoured cars, the Specials launched an attack on the Catholic streets in Millfield firing indiscriminately into homes.

Houses in Boyd Street and California Street were burned and families forced to flee.

Several people died and many were wounded in the attacks which spread to other districts. The Millfield attack culminated in an attack on St. Mary's presbytery.

Woods reported that most of the I.R.A. officers, including Company Captains, were attending a Brigade meeting when the attacks took place and the moral of the Catholic people in the area was nearly broken.

The report also describes deterioration in Company areas despite their burning campaign and shows the first signs of real moral problems within the Belfast Brigade by June 1922.

Woods continues:

"Several of our dumps have been captured within the last few weeks and in practically every case the raiding party went direct to the house. In many of these raids, Company and Battalion papers have been found with the result that many officers and men are forced to go on the run necessarily in their own restricted areas. They find it difficult to get accommodation with the people now and in a particular area, seventeen of our best officers and men had to sleep in a refugee's home where they were all captured. As I mentioned before, the economic position is very acute."

"To give a rough idea, there are 171 married men with 405 dependents and 346 single men with 936 dependents."

"These figures are taken from cards returned by each Company."

It is clear from Seamus Woods report that senior figures within the Dail had turned their back on the north in pursuit of the growing problems arising in the south over the treaty.

This fact is recognised by Woods when in another detailed report seven days later, he says:

"the people who supported us feel Dail Eireann has abandoned them. They feel that all their suffering has been in vain and cannot see any hope for the future."

Events after the death of Michael Collins would prove as such, with Mulcahy, Collin's successor and Cosgrave's government cutting the lifeline to the Northern Divisions and adopting a *"peace policy"* with the Northern Parliament.

Divisional Staff - 1921. Seamus Woods seated left of picture.

The vast majority of the I.R.A. in the north had remained loyal to the Provisional Government GHQ. This was in part a reflection of the immense organizational and operational difficulties created by the presence of a large Unionist population and the reliance of the minority, especially in Belfast, on the moral and material support of the Provisional Government.

Seamus Woods had back in April convinced the majority of the men under his command that by supporting the Provisional Government and the treaty that there was a better chance of: *"**overcoming the position in the north**".*

"The Phoenix had risen from the flames."

The final blow against overcoming the position that Seamus Woods made reference to, came with the death of Michael Collins in August 1922 and the resulting underhand politics from the new Free State government that resulted in a change of policy toward the north. This effectively spelt the end of the northern I.R.A.

Only the 4th Northern Division that operated in the South Armagh and County Louth areas remained as an effective fighting group in a good state of strength

Woods in the end became so sufficiently disillusioned with the Cosgrave administration and the betrayal of his Division, that he asked GHQ to relieve him of his anomalous commission.

Despite a new resurgence in the mid-thirties by the I.R.A. in Belfast, it would be 48 years before they would once more be able to strike at the heart of the Unionist State. This time it would not be a short sharp campaign reliant on Dublin support, but an all out assault of guerrilla warfare that would spell the end of Unionist domination in the north. That assault would begin on the streets of the Short Strand during the night of the 27th June 1970, the very district that Loyalists had tried to erase from the geographical landscape of East Belfast during the 1920-1922 years of conflict and pogrom

UNDERHAND POLITICS AND BETRAYAL

Seamus Woods report to GHQ written on the 20th July, 1922, highlights the frustration and concern in relation to the poor state of moral at that point within the Belfast Brigade.

His persistence was rewarded when the Northern Commanders were called to a conference at Portobello Barracks in Dublin on the 2nd August, 1922 to consider the whole position of the Pro-Treaty I.R.A. in the north.

The urgency of the conference had been emphasised by the defection of Frank Aiken and his 4th Northern Division to the Executive-[Anti-Treaty] Forces.

Aiken's earlier policy was one of trying to maintain a neutral standing. He believed it was *"bad tactics"* to fight against each other.

In a letter to the Minister for Defence-[Michael Collins] on the 6th July, 1922, he told him *"that if ordered, I would not attack the Executive Forces, but on the other hand, I thought the Executive should quit."*

After a meeting with Liam Lynch, Commander of the Executive Forces on the 8th July, Aiken returned to his HQ in Dundalk, were orders awaited him from GHQ, to report with his staff to Dublin and to issue orders to his Division to begin attacks on the Executive.

Aiken, decided to assemble all his Staff, Brigade and Battalion Commanders-[including Executive] to a meeting on Friday, 14th July, 1922.

It was agreed to keep the Divisional organisation intact along Volunteer lines until attacks in the north could continue and that all war material be concealed within the Divisional area.

At Portobello, on 2nd August, Michael Collins, concerned at the course of events taken by Aiken, moved to keep the other Divisions on board.

For him, a unified "Army" was paramount. No matter what the politicians wanted, that was his priority.

Collins was due to leave Dublin for a tour of inspection in his native West Cork and he assured his northern comrades that:

"the government in Dublin intended to deal with the Ulster situation in a very definite way"

A number of firm decisions were made concerning the I.R.A. in the north. It was agreed that the I.R.A. volunteers who could not remain in the six-county area would be trained in the Curragh under their own officers in guerrilla warfare and that finance would be provided for the continued payment of Divisional Staff and intelligence work.

The northern commanders in attendance were:

- Seamus Woods   O/C 3rd Northern
- Rodger Mc Corley-Vice   O/C 3rd Northern
- Tom Morris   O/C 2nd Northern
- J.Mallin Q/M-2nd Northern
- J.Casey 2I/C Newry Brigade, 4th Northern

They would all have been greatly heartened by the result of that meeting. It is worth noting the presence of the 4th Northern officer.

In one of Seamus Woods last reports to GHQ on the 29th September, 1922, Woods makes reference to the 2nd August meeting, clarifying Collins position regarding the north.

> **"On August 2nd the meeting was held and the late Commander in Chief-[Michael Collins] presided. At that meeting the situation in the Six Counties was discussed at great length, with the view to improving our organization and training and for a policy to be adopted by our people in the north, which would have the sanction of the government in Dublin."**

> **"The late C.I.C made it clear to us that the government in Dublin intended to deal with the Ulster situation in a very definite way and as far as this Division was concerned, every officer present felt greatly encouraged to carry on the work when we had a definite policy to pursue and an assurance that the government here would stand by us."**

By the end of August 1922, 379 men including volunteers from B Company, had arrived at the Curragh under the "so-called" training scheme.

Unknown to the northern officers who left Portobello Barracks after the August 2nd meeting feeling a new optimistic, they were in a false position.

Ernest Blythe.

While Michael Collins was genuine in his efforts to support the north and create a policy of direction for the Northern Divisions, others within the Provisional Government were pursuing a different agenda.

The day before the Portobello meeting, the government in Dublin appointed a committee to explore how it could shape a fundamental change in its Ulster policy.

Mulcahy, who was present at the Portobello meeting, knew of this and he recorded at the meeting that a *"peace policy* [was] *essential"*

The architect of the new northern policy was Ernest Blythe.

He rejected any continuation of an *"aggressive policy"* involving either physical coercion or economic pressure, which he considered counter-productive.. He recommended that on receiving British assurances, the Northern Divisions should be urged to disarm.

Blythe's views were taken on board by the committee and on the 19th August 1922, the Provisional Government formally adopted *"a peace policy"* with the Northern Parliament

Michael Collins is often illustrated as the image of the Free State and its forces after the signing of the treaty. He was a charismatic figure who embodied the whole concept of Irish Resistance and many photographs of Collins in uniform depict this image. He took great pride in his role as Commander in Chief of the new National Army-[so called], but behind this public image was a man who felt a deep sense of dismay over the split within the I.R.A. and for the six northern counties.

Collins was very aware that the treaty he had helped to broker and deliver had cut off the north from the rest of the country, leaving its Nationalist inhabitants feeling isolated and betrayed.

Two of the three Northern Divisions had remained loyal to the Provisional Government; in reality they had little choice as their lifeline led south.

Collins fed that lifeline ensuring the I.R.A. in the north received weapons to foremost defend the Nationalist districts, but also to enable them to carry out offensive operations.

It was also Collins who gave the directive for the assassination of Field Marshall Sir Henry Wilson in London on the 22nd June 1922.

Although the evidence is inconclusive, the balance of probability is that Collins, outraged by the "excesses and murders" being carried out against the Catholics in the north, to which Wilson, a member of the British Parliament, had recently been appointed military advisor, had him executed.

The cabinet in Dublin was appalled at Wilson's killing, which Collins had ordered without their knowledge.

But while the William Cosgrave led government was condemning and deploring the deed, Collins was consulting with Liam Lynch and Rory O' Conner, leaders of the Executive forces, as to the possibility of their being able to assist in a rescue attempt of the two men responsible. Both had been captured after the shooting.

Reginald Dunne and Joseph O' Sullivan, both British Army veterans were held in Wandsworth Gaol, but no plan that would succeed could be put in place quickly enough and they were both later hanged.

The killing of Henry Wilson was a turning point in many ways **and this, rather than the treaty, may have sealed Michael Collins fate.**

Firstly, it incensed the British who dictated that the Free State Forces move against the Executive Forces who had occupied the Four Courts in Dublin.

Secondly, it caused Collins to leave the cabinet and focus on his role as Chief of Staff.

Collins, until his death, attended meetings of the cabinet despite their critical attitude toward him for not always following their directives.

He had lost the confidence of the cabinet and he in turn had no faith in them, in particular the hawks; Desmond Fitzgerald, Ernest Blythe and Kevin O' Higgins.

The day, the civil war officially began, 27th June 1922 with the shelling of The Four Courts by Free State troops using British field guns, the last shipment of weapons left the Courts for the north via Donegal

One unusual event is worth highlighting.

Within weeks of the shelling of the Four Courts, Kevin O Higgins was appointed to an army post and he transferred from his government post to Portobello Barracks, Collin's HQ.

Kevin O' Higgins was not a military man and was one of those that Collins needed to be wary off within the cabinet.

He sought tough action against Republican forces and his appointment to a military post at Portobello may also have included an ability to observe Collins activities at source. *

Kevin O'Higgins (UCD)

The following month, the death of Michael Collins on the 22nd August 1922 on a narrow road at *Béal na mBláth* in West Cork, made all the hopes, the maybes and*" the what could have happened if*" ... conversations, irrelevant.

The death of Michael Collins, spelt the death of the Northern Divisions.

Ironically, it was O' Higgins who received the encoded message from Emmet Dalton in Cork City of Collins death.

Collins still to this day provokes much interest and debate in Irish history. Like all great characters of history there is a sense of aura, a mystique person whose image portrays everything that is the embodiment of Ireland's conflict during this period.

In reality he was a man who fitted the hour and used his strength of character to pursue his objectives. Despite the romantic image, Collins was ruthless in implementing those objectives and done what he considered necessary in achieving what needed done. He was suited to the period and deserves his standing in history.

For decades controversy has surrounded his death. Various theories of murder and British involvement have been put forward which have been countered by those who believe he died from *"a republican bullet"* during the *Béal na mBláth* ambush, which is the official version of his death.

Many historians prefer to endorse the official version; others do not and therefore the Collins "legend" remains very much alive to this day.

Was Collins death the culmination of a concerted campaign to remove him from the scene, directed by "Irishmen" who feared his efforts to end the civil war and reunite the I.R.A. as a National Army to regroup, reorganise and look north ?

Collins death allowed the new cabinet policy of the 2nd August as constructed by Ernest Blythe to be implemented.

Mulcahy took over as Chief of Staff and launched a bloody purge against Republican Forces, which included roadside murders of prisoners, atrocities and executions at the behest of military courts.

Some of these actions were nothing short of war crimes carried out by the so-called NATIONAL ARMY under the direction of the government.

Richard Mulcahy

Collin's assassination escalated the civil war, a war in which Collins in his own words to Captain Sean Mc Carthy during the final days of his life expressed a deep desire to bring to an end.

"I am going to put an end to this bloody war as quickly as possible"

His killing allowed those that he described as **"Spies and traitors**" to escalate a war and create bloodshed and murder that would surpass anything the *"Black and Tans"* carried out.

Sir Neville Mc Cready, the G.O.C. of British Forces in Ireland between 1918 and 1920, said **"that the pro-treaty forces had achieved victory by means far more drastic than any which the British Government dared to impose during the worst period of rebellion."**

Eighty-two men were executed within ten months by the Free State. The deeds and atrocities carried out by the Cosgrave administration of Fitzgerald, O Higgins, Blythe and Mulcahy, were in stark contrast to the ideals of the men of 1916.

They murdered their own and deprived Ireland of one of its greatest modern leaders.

The Cosgrave government made no hurried move to disband the Northern I.R.A. Divisions after the death of Michael Collins for fear of their defection to the Executive Forces. Policy was designed to absorb the northerners into the Free State Army, while providing a special fund for the relief of Pro-Treaty volunteers in Wood's Divisional area.

This decision was taken in October 1922 and Seamus Woods was informed on the 22nd December.

However Seamus Woods remained unhappy with the evasive answers he received from Mulcahy about future policy regarding the Northern I.R.A., while he shared his men's anger at the Free State execution of Joe Mc Kelvey-[Vice Chief of Staff of the Executive Forces] on the 8th December 1922.

Mulcahy had already declined a request from Woods in October to explain the position in relation to Northern I.R.A. officers, stating merely that government policy on the north **"is the policy of the treaty"**

By 5th January 1923, Seamus Woods was sufficiently disillusioned to request GHQ to relieve him of his command.

He was subsequently captured by the Unionist authorities.

In the resulting uncertainty, Northern I.R.A. men at the Curragh either applied to join the Free State Army, or simply "went home".

The Northern Divisions were officially disbanded on the 31st March 1923.

This whole episode of events was to have much more far reaching consequences upon the six northern counties, the price of which was paid in blood some fifty years later and at a much higher rate than experienced during the 1919-1922 period, which cast independence for 26 of Ireland's 32 counties and not *"The Republic of 1916."*

*[Kevin O' Higgins was shot and killed by the I.R.A. in 1927]

Left to Right:
Joe McHenry, Andy Cooney, Joe McKelvey
This photograph was taken in Mountjoy Gaol on the 7th December 1922 the day before Joe McKelvey's reprisal execution by Free State Forces [*Kilmainham archive*]

Sir Henry Wilson

POST CONFLICT RE-ORGANIZATION OF THE I.R.A.

Following the *"dump arms"* order of the 24th May 1923, a complete re-organization of Óglaigh na hÉireann began under Chief of Staff Frank Aiken.

Aiken had brought the civil war to an end on the 30th April 1923, when as Chief of Staff he had called a ceasefire and ordered his men to *"dump arms"*.

Frank Aiken originated from the town land of *Carrickbracken,* Camlough in South Armagh and as the O/C of the 4th Northern Division which covered South Armagh, North Louth and South Down; he proved an efficient and equally, a ruthless leader in his area of operations.

South Armagh became a fertile killing ground with reprisal and counter-reprisal killings between the I.R.A. under Aiken and the B.Specials.

He also targeted R.I.C. barracks and operated from what Aiken himself described as ***"our loyal allies, the hills".***

Amid ambushes on Specials, Aiken's men burned the homes and farms of Orange Order members in County Armagh.

One date that stands out in the memory of Protestants from the county, is the 17th June 1922, the date of which is termed the *"Altnagelvin Massacre"*, when seven Protestants one a Special, were shot and killed by the I.R.A. who, 50 strong, raided and burned Protestant homes.

Two months later, having decided to side with the Executive Forces at the outbreak of the civil war, he moved against his old HQ in Dundalk which had been occupied by Free State troops.

In "textbook" military terms, it was a perfect operation resulting in the barrack being captured and 200 Executive Volunteers being released from imprisonment.

Sinn Fein, now under the leadership of Eamon Donnelly, returned 44 Abstentionist candidates in the second Free State elections of 1924, rising to 48 candidates, due to By-Elections.

In the north and in Belfast, the I.R.A. was in a poor state and needed to completely reform; many volunteers had gone south to serve in the Free State Army or had been forced to emigrate due to unemployment within a hostile Unionist State.

Others were expelled either to the Free State, or England.

For those who remained, training and re-organization began slowly, spearheaded by the release of Internees, although many of them were served with *"expulsion orders"* from the Six-Counties.

In some areas, training was conducted under the guise of Gaelic Athletic Clubs, as the aim of reforming the Belfast Battalion-[Not a Brigade] was underway under the leadership of Hugh Corvin , a former Brigade officer.

One of the first meetings to take place occurred in a room above a small bookshop on the corner of Marquis and Castle Street.

It was here that D Company which covered the Pound Loney/Divis area of Belfast was resurrected. The last O/C of the Belfast Brigade, Arthur Thornbury, along with other 3rd Northern Volunteers would be on hand to help in the reconstruction.

Arms dumps were sought out in districts such as Ballymacarrett and lifted for potential training. I.R.A. strength in Belfast was *at an all-time low*

Many of the experienced officers were now in the Free State Army or living out of the state. But despite continued state persecution, the I.R.A. was functioning again, even if it was at a low level.

Several men from the district were arrested and charged with possession of arms and ammunition during 1924/1925.

Willy Devlin of Vulcan Street was charged with possession of a pistol and ammunition in 1924.

The following year, John Connolly of Thompson Street, Dan Mc Gurk of Chemical Street, Joe Mc Clelland, of Anderson Street and John Walsh of Chemical Street, were charged at various dates throughout the year following raids into the district by the RUC and Specials.

The **Special Powers Act** was used to arrest men for *"membership of an unlawful association"*.

Prominent within the Battalion were the Matthew Brothers, Davy and Hugh.

On the 11th August 1923, the RUC acting on information received * discovered a haul of ammunition at the Anderson Felt Works on the Short Strand. The find consisted of:

A webley [MK V1] revolver; 900 rounds of .303 ammunition-[MKV1 and MKV11] ; 200 rounds of assorted revolver ammunition ; 9 Mills grenades-[rusted] and 1 egg pattern bomb.

This find was the first of three to be uncovered at the same location between August 1923 and January 1925. All of the material dated back to the 1920-1922 period and had remained undetected during the crucial period of the fighting.

It may not necessarily have been in that location at the time, but its discovery would have been a blow to a fledging IRA trying to reform itself during the early-mid twenties.

A year later on the night of 18th September 1924, an RUC raiding party from Mountpottinger barrack under District Inspector Spears were called to the factory by the manager who told them that ammunition and bombs had been discovered in a store by a workman. The find included:

96 rounds of automatic ammunition [German] ; 74 rounds of .303 ammunition ; 7 rounds of .455 ammunition ; 6 Mills grenades and a canister of detonators.
The following morning the RUC returned to the factory as a .303 rifle and bayonet had also been recovered.
Raids were carried out by the RUC and Specials into the district.

In a secret follow up RUC report from the Commissioners office it was stated that

Raids took place in what it states *" In the Sinn Fein area of this district, where it was thought further arms might be found, but without success. These arms are the property of the local IRA and as no local rebels could be connected with this find, no arrests were made."*

[The reference of *"rebels"* is a terminology I came across previous in a report written from Mountpottinger Barrack by DI Spears regarding the arrest of Hamilton Young and highlights the sectarian nature of the RUC]

During the conflict period of 1920-1922, despite numerous raids within the district, weapons dumps in the main remained undetected. There were a few finds uncovered such as in Seaforde Street in October 1922, when the conflict period had more or less ended.
One important location in the Seaforde Street area and another close to the church remained undetected during the crucial period.

*[The reference in the 1923 RUC report of "From information received", does not necessarily indicate an informer as the same was said regarding the September 1924 find.]

On the broad political front, following the Sinn Fein *Ard Fheis* of the 9th March 1926, Eamon de Valera resigned as President of Sinn Fein, due to a difference of policy and direction.

A couple of weeks later, De Valera announced the formation of a new party called Fianna Fail [Republican Party] whose aims he outlined as:

Securing the political independence of the whole island as a republic.

- Restoring the Irish Language
- Developing a social system affording equal opportunities to every Irish citizen to live a noble and useful Christian life.
- The redistribution of land in order to get the greatest number of Irish families possible rooted in the soil and making Ireland as economically self-contained and self-sufficient as it could be.

Fianna Fail was officially launched at the *La Scala* theatre on Prince's Street in Dublin on the 26th May 1926 with De Valera being elected as President

De Valera explained at the time that Fianna Fail's immediate aim was to remove the oath and once this was done, it would be possible to advance the national cause by *"cutting the bonds of foreign interference one by one until the full internal sovereignty of the Twenty-Six counties was established beyond question."*

"With a united Twenty-Six counties", he added, *"the position would be reached in which the solution of the problem of successfully bringing in the north could be confidently undertaken."*

Entering the Dail entailed recognizing the existence of partition, but he contended that this did not mean they would be endorsing it.

"*To recognize the existence of the facts, as we must, is not to acquiesce to them*" he declared. "*We shall at all times be morally free to use any means that God gives us to reunite the country and win back the part of our Ulster Province that has been taken away from us.*"

De Valera was bringing to a fine art the process of acting constitutionally while cloaking his actions in revolutionary rhetoric.

On the 29th June 1926, a month after the formation of Fianna Fail, he said at a rally in Clare: "*I stand for an Irish Republic, for all the full freedom of Ireland, as thoroughly today as I stood nine years ago when I first came before you*".

While Fianna Fail Cumans sprang up all over the Twenty-Six counties, De Valera was making off with Sinn Fein's Republican emotional narrative.

De Valera travelled extensively helping to build support for the new party and embarked on two fund raising trips to the United States, firstly in March 1927 and again in December 1929.

Following victory in the election held on the 9th March 1932, Fianna Fail entered the Dail and Eamon De Valera was once again elected President of Dail Eireann.

Nine years after their defeat in the civil war, a "*Republican Party*" was once more in power in the Free State. Those who carried the mantle of the anti-treaty forces during the civil war had now turned military defeat into political victory.

 Before Finn Gael handed over power, they ordered all secret papers to be burned, which included files relating to the civil war and the death of Michael Collins.

Throughout the thirties, De Valera undid most of what Republicans felt to be unacceptable about the 1921 treaty.

These included: Land annuity payments to Britain, the oath of allegiance to the British Crown, the Office of Governor General, the right of appeal to the Privy Council, British access to Irish Naval facilities and the 1922 constitution.

The new government under De Valera, although still professing itself as a Republican Party, moved away from the concept of armed struggle and having used the I.R.A. to gain control of the country, now proscribed the I.R.A.

De Valera split the Republican Movement by offering pensions and appointments in what was a Twenty-Six county state, not an all-Ireland Irish Republic.

He was "officially" closing the door to armed struggle.

Those who accepted entered the establishment and just as in 1922, those who remained loyal to the Republic were outlawed and persecuted.

De Valera contributed greatly in tearing the I.R.A. apart at a time when it had regained its strength following the civil war. He took away its political soul in order to pursue *"his political aims"*.

His actions contributed in cementing partition, the very thing he pledged to dismantle in his political rhetoric.

His government broke the strength of the I.R.A. in the south by enticing Republicans into a Free State Army in order to isolate *"Militant Republicanism"*

Men such as Frank Aiken entered the establishment and he became the new Minister of Defence opposing any I.R.A. activity.

Military tribunals were re-established on the 22nd August 1933 and in November of the same year, a new volunteer force was established [today's F.C.A. - Army Reserve] all designed to break up the I.R.A.

Republicanism was now more a tool of traditional propaganda than any move militant or otherwise toward unification.

The one positive and highly significant development to emerge from the Fianna Fail government came about on the 10th March 1937, when it introduced a new constitution to *An Dail*, which became law the following year.

Within that constitution would be the clause defining Ireland as:

"The whole island of Ireland, its islands and its territorial seas."

The terms Saorstat Eireann/Irish Free State were removed and replaced by Eire/Ireland.

The military courts were abolished and I.R.A. prisoners released.

The I.R.A. in the thirties epically in the Twenty-Six counties had no real notion of direction. Only in Belfast did it find a role during outbreaks of sectarian violence when it acted as a form of defence in Nationalist districts such as in July 1935, during which the Ballymacarrett Company played a prominent role in the defence of Lancaster Street/York Street area

Overall, despite its forays, parades and Company strengths in Belfast, it was lacking clear policy and direction until 1938. In the south, it was purely a policy of agitation toward state aggression.

THE FOLLOWING LISTING IS A MAKE UP OF THE REPUBLICAN MOVEMENT IN BALLYMACARRETT AS AT 1937. NOT ALL THOSE LISTED WERE ACTIVE WITHIN B COMPANY AT THE TIME, BUT WERE REPUBLICANS AND SUSPECTED BY RUC INTELLIGENCE AS MEMBERS OF THE IRA.

JOSEPH BOLES	80 SEAFORDE STREET
JACK BRADY	KILMOOD STREET- [Company O/C]
GERARD CURRAN	205 MOUNTPOTTINGER ROAD
KEVIN CURRAN	205 MOUNTPOTTINGER ROAD
FRANCIS CAMPBELL	38 CHEMICAL STREET
FELIX DEVLIN	13 LOWRY STREET
JOHN DEVLIN	13 LOWRY STREET
PATRICK DIGNAN	30 ANDERSON STREET
DANIEL DOHERTY	47 SHERIFF STREET
STEPHEN DUFFY	10 THOMPSON STREET
JAMES FARRELLY	31 VULCAN STREET
JOHN FARRELLY	31 VULCAN STREET
BERNARD FOX	65 SHERIFF STREET
GERARD GREENAN	18 SAUL STREET
JIM HARVEY	34 KILMOOD STREET
CATHERINE HENDRON	18 ALTCAR STREET-[Cumann na mBan]
JOHN KEENAN	43 SHORT STRAND
MICHAEL KEENAN	43 SHORT STRAND
HUGH KEENAN	32 SHORT STRAND
JOHN MC AVOY	25 SHERIFF STREET
GERARD MC CLINTON	41 MADRID STREET
RICHARD MC DERMOTT	49 KILMOOD STREET
PATRICK MC KENNA	10 FOUNDRY STREET

WILLIAM MC KENNA   10 FOUNDRY STREET

LIAM MC KENNA   49 SEAFORDE STREET

PATRICK MC KEOWN   17 BEECHFIELD STREET

HENRY MC NEILLY   65 THOMPSON STREET

ROBERT MC MILLIAN   20 MOIRA STREET

JOSEPH MORROW   WOODSTOCK STREET

JAMES MULHOLLAND   50 CHEMICAL STREET

JOHN MULLIGAN   5 MADRID STREET

PATRICK MULLIGAN   58 MADRID STREET

WILLIAM MURRAY   66 CHEMICAL STREET

JOSEPH MURRAY   67 MOUNTPOTTINGER ROAD

GERARD MURRAY   67 MOUNTPOTTINGER ROAD

JOHN NOAD   56 CLYDE STREET

WILLIAM O HANLON   13 WOODSTOCK STREET- [Went to fight in Spain 1937]

PATRICK O NEILL   30 KILMOOD STREET

BERNARD ROONEY   71 THOMPSON STREET

PATRICK ROONEY   45 THOMPSON STREET

MULES SMITH   29 SHERIFF STREET

JAMES STRANNEY   57 THOMPSON STREET-[Company Q.M, but left to fight in Spain]

PATRICK THOMPSON   8 ARRAN STREET

MICHAEL WALSH   30 CHEMICAL STREET

DENIS WHELEN   97 BRIDGE END

THOMAS WHINERY   24 CHEMICAL STREET

[This listing is by no means definitive and additional names would be welcome]

FOOTNOTES

B - [BALLYMACARRETT], COMPANY, 2nd BATTALION,

BELFAST BRIGADE, IRISH REPUBLICAN ARMY.

As at the date of the truce, 11th July, 1921, the Belfast Brigade's 2nd Battalion had a nominal role of 303 men.

The Battalion O/C was **Rory Mc Nicholl**, the Adjutant was **Joe Mc Peake** from Little May Street; he later became a Captain in the Free State Army and **Seamus Keating** was the Battalion Q.M.

B – [Ballymacarrett] Company comprised of 88-90 Volunteers.

The Company Captain and O/C was **John-[Sean] Cunningham** of 43 Comber Street.

A former regular soldier with 8 years pre-war service, he served again throughout WW1 before joining the I.R.A.

Company 2 I/C was James Rice.

Company Adjutant was Lieutenant Joseph Cassidy from Kilmood Street

John Cunningham became a Commandant in the Free State Army until his retirement in 1929. He later joined O Duffy's Nationalist Volunteers during the Spanish Civil War, but remained a Republican until his death in Belfast aged 79 on the 8th March 1963. He is buried in Milltown Cemetery-DB-309.B

James Rice of Foundry Street became an opponent of the treaty and later went to the USA.

Joseph Cassidy of 49 Kilmood Street became a Captain in the Free State Army based in Dublin.

John Duggan, 87 Short Strand served in the 14th Battalion [YCV], Royal Irish Rifles. He enlisted in January 1915 and served throughout the war until he was wounded on the 10th June, 1917. Corporal Duggan was sent home on the 15th June due to the extent of his wounds. He is listed on B Company's nominal role.

Richard Curran, 25 Kilmood Street who served in the Connaught Rangers during WW1, was awarded the MM-Military Medal, in 1917 for bravery, and is listed on B Company's nominal role.

Private B Hughes of 6, Khartoum Street served in the Irish Guards during WW1 and was awarded the MM-Military Medal for bravery.

There is a J.Hughes and C.Hughes of Khartoum Street listed on B Company's nominal role.

Michael Gargin of Thompson Street served in the Royal Irish Rifles during WW1 and was taken POW.

He was interned by the Northern regime in 1922.

Private J.Copeland of 54 Sheriff Street served in the Royal Irish Fusiliers and was killed on the 25th April, 1915 at Hill 60 during the 1st Battle of Ypres. He had 16 years' service in the British Army and had previously saw action in the Boer War. Prior to his death, he was awarded the DCM-Distinguished Conduct Medal for conspicuous bravery at *Armentieres.*

Edward Copeland of 65 Sheriff Street—[Brother/Son-?] is listed on B Company's nominal role.

Francis Bradley, 13 Khartoum Street is listed on B Company's nominal role.

John Bradley, also of 13 Khartoum Street served in the British Army during WW1.

Private R. J. Dixon, 11 Saul Street served during WW1 in the Royal Irish Rifles and was badly wounded. His brother Thomas also of 11 Saul Street was possibly a member of B Company [research on-going].

Hamilton Young of 13 Saul Street served in the British Army during WW1. He enlisted at the outbreak of war and was deployed to France on the 3rd February 1915 with the 2nd Battalion Royal Irish Rifles. He later served with the 6th Battalion of the same regiment and later with the Leinsters. He joined B Company in 1920. He was an active volunteer throughout 1920 and 1921, but was arrested in November 1921 and sentenced to 9 months imprisonment. Upon his release on the 18th July, 1922, as with the majority of volunteers he went down south to be amalgamated into the Free State Army for what they believed was to be a future renewal of the campaign in the north. He was sent back to the north by his old Company Captain, John Cunningham, to ensure any weapons in the Battalion area, did not fall into the hands of the Anti-Treaty faction.

Despite carrying a letter of authorisation signed by Cunningham, he was arrested on the 8th September, 1922 by the Northern authorities and interned. He was held in Internment for the next 2 years and despite his young daughter, Ellen dying, his wife, Edith, being in poor health, they refused to release him.

RUC intelligence papers state:

"He was a dangerous I.R.A. man and took a leading and fearless part in the outrages committed by them. His release is not recommended."

He was eventually released on the 15th December, 1924, having been held on the Prison Ship *Argenta* and in Derry Gaol.

J.Moan -wounded on the 9th May 1915 while serving in the Royal Irish Rifles. There is a **H.Moan** listed on B Company's nominal role.

Richard Curran, 25 Kilmood Street who served in the Connaught Rangers during WW1, was awarded the MM-Military Medal, in 1917 for bravery, and is listed on B Company's nominal role.

James Gibbons, 42 Seaforde Street served in the Royal Inniskilling Fusiliers during WW1 He became a POW. James is listed on B Company's nominal role and following his release from Internment, moved to Derry.

Billy Murray of 66 Chemical St.
(photographed in later years)
He was Interned by the Northern authorities both in
the 1920s and 1940s.

(Photo credit Bernie Murray)

INTERNMENT ORDER.

the Inspect

WHEREAS it appears to me, on the recommendation of ᵡᶜᵡⁱⁿᵗⁿᵗⁱ
R.U.C. that for securing the preservation of the peace and the mainten

rder in Northern Ireland, it is expedient that

WM. F. MURRAY.

f 66 Chemical Street, Belfast.

n the County of ------

ho is suspected of being about to act in a manner prejudicial to the pre

f the peace and ance of order in Northern Ireland, s

TRANSFER INTERNMENT ORDER.

Transfer .... day

WHEREAS by an Internment Order dated ......18th..............

of ......OCTOBER, 1923............ made by me in virtue of the

powers vested in me by the Civil Authorities (Special Powers)

Act (Northern Ireland) 1922, and the Regulations made

thereunder and of all other powers me thereunto enabling

......WILLIAM F. MURRAY,.................... of ..66. CHEMICAL STREET...

......BELFAST.. was ordered to be

interned in ......H.M. PRISON, LONDONDERRY...................................

NOW, I, THE RIGHT HONOURABLE SIR RICHARD DAWSON BATES,

Minister of Home Affairs for Northern Ireland, by virtue

of the powers vested in me by the Act and Regulations afore-

BALLYMACARRETT ARGENTA INTERNEES

RICHARD ARMOUR

CHARLES BURNS

DAVID BENNETT

PATRICK DEVLIN

JAMES GIBBONS

PATRICK KANE

JAMES HERON

JOSEPH FLANNIGAN

JAMES MC GOURAN

JOSEPH MC CLELLAND

WILLIAM MC CONNELL

WILLIAM MURRAY

HAMILTON YOUNG

FRED YOUNG

RICHARD RYAN

JOSEPH MC DERMOTT

JOHN STEENSON

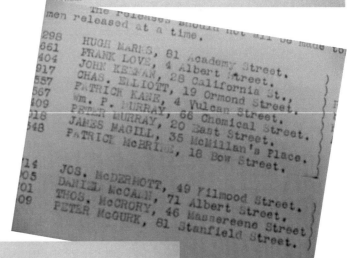

B (BALLYMACARRETT} COMPANY, 2nd BATTALION, BELFAST BRIGADE

3rd NORTHERN DIVISION, IRISH REPUBLICAN ARMY

1920-1922

COMPANY STAFF

The first O/C of B Company when it was raised in 1920, was Donegal man, Captain **Manus O Boyle** who was working and living in Belfast He first arrived in Belfast from London in early March 1916 to avoid conscription into the British Army. Already a member of the IRB and Volunteer Movement, he continued his membership in Belfast.

Sean O Neill, a former Sergeant Major in the Irish Guards was in charge of training. Manus struck up a friendship with Seamus Dobbyn and Liam Gaynor and participated in the unsuccessful attempt by the Belfast Volunteers to take part in the rising during Easter week

Following the creation of the I.R.A. in Belfast in 1917, he joined B Company, 1st Battalion in which Joe Mc Kelvey was a Section Leader.

The first O/C of what was then the Belfast Battalion was Sean Cusack also a former soldier.

After various jobs, Manus was working as a cashier in the Chemical works in the Short Strand, when he was asked by the Brigade Staff to become Captain of a new Company being raised in Ballymacarrett in 1920 as part of forming a 2nd Battalion, with Tom Fitzpatrick as O/C.

Tom Fitzpatrick, a WW1 veteran was originally from County Cavan. He first joined the I.R.A. in August 1919, as a member of C Company, Belfast Battalion based in the Divis area. When the O/C Seamus Keating fell into bad health, Tom took over the Company.

John {Sean} Cunningham-Company 2/IC –{later to become O/C}

The new Ballymacarrett Company

was designated **B Company, 2nd Battalion**

Helping Manus O Boyle was his 2I/C, **John {Sean} Cunningham** of Comber Street, a former regular soldier in the British Army and WW1 veteran.

John Cunningham was born in August 1884 in Ballynahinch, Co. Down

He enlisted in the British Army on the 3rd September, 1904 at 19 years of age

His service lasted for eight years and he returned to live in Belfast settling in Ballymacarrett, were he married Catherine O' Hare from Bryson Street in St. Matthews church on the 3rd May,1913.

At the outbreak of WW1, he re-enlisted, serving with the Royal Dragoon Guards and served throughout the war, first in France and later the Middle East.

At the outbreak of the conflict in Belfast in 1920, John Cunningham, now living at 43 Comber Street, became 2I/C of the new I.R.A. Company in Ballymacarrett.

He succeeded Manus O'Boyle, as Company OC and remained as OC through the truce period.

John Cunningham transferred into the new Free State Army in 1922, with the rank of Commandant, he was in command of the 49th Battalion based in Dundalk.

In November 1923, he transferred to Collins Barracks in Dublin, where he became OC of the 21st Battalion on the 1st October 1924.

He retired from the Free State Army in 1929.

A few years later, while living back in Belfast, he renewed his acquaintance with Eoin O'Duffy and joined the Nationalist Volunteers raised in support of General Franco, during the Spanish Civil War-{1936-1939}.

With a commission in the 15th Bandera *Irlandesa del Tercio*, he sailed to Spain for what became an ill-fated and undistinguished 6 month period for the Nationalist Volunteers.

John Cunningham resigned his commission on the 6th April, 1937, returning to Ireland and his home town of Belfast.

He settled back into civilian life but maintained his republican links.

At Easter 1939, he led the I.R.A. veterans' annual Easter Sunday parade to Milltown Cemetery.

In 1948, John Cunningham led the Ballymacarrett contingent in the 1798 centenary commemoration parade.

His role as a republican and his contribution to the Republican Movement has been wrongly overshadowed by his conservative thinking and involvement in Spain with the Nationalist contingent.

John {Sean} Cunningham, died on the 8th March, 1963 aged 79 and was buried in Milltown Cemetery, Belfast with republican honours.

James Rice - was the Company 2I/C under John Cunningham.

He was active with the Company throughout the two years of conflict, but unlike his fellow officers he opposed the treaty and did not join the Free State Army.

He took command of the small anti-treaty unit in Ballymacarrett, with Charles Burns as his 2I/C.

Like so many who opposed the treaty, he had to leave the country following the Civil War and immigrated to the United States.

Joseph Cassidy, 49 Kilmood Streeet. The Company Adjutant under John Cunningham. He joined the Free State Army in 1922, holding the rank of Captain, based in Dublin.

Manus O'Boyle taken in later years in his home village of MountCharles Co Donegal.

LISTING OF VOLUNTEERS AS AT THE TRUCE PERIOD JULY 1921

ARMOUR, RICHARD.......... [GLENHOLMES], Vulcan St.

BENNETT, DAVID .... 69 Anderson Street

CHARLES BURNS............... Altcar Street,

FRANCIS BRADLEY .... 13 Khartoum Street

J.CAMPBELL....................... Anderson Street

C.CAMPBELL .... Kilmood Street

R,CAMPBELL .... Mountpottinger Road

WILLIAM CARLIN .... 7 Arran Street

T.CONNOLLY..................... ?

EDWARD COPELAND........ 65 Sheriff Street

J.CORRY .... Seaforde Street

FRANCIS CULLEN .... 8 Foundry Street

RICHARD CURRAN .... 25 Kilmood Street

JAMES CURRAN................ 29 Lowry Street

JOSEPH CURRAN .... 67 Sheriff Street

PATRICK DEVLIN .... 13 Lowry Street

JOHN DUGGAN................. 87 Short Strand

M.DUNN .... Beechfield Street

B.FEE................................. Chemical Street

JAMES FITZPATRICK .... Middlepath Street

JOHN FLANNAGAN .... Kilmood Street

R.GEORGE......................... Mountpottinger Road

J.GIBNEY .... Comber Street

JAMES GIBBONS............... 42 Seaforde Street

J.GLENN .... ?

P.GORMAN....................... Beechfield Street

D or E.GRAHAME.............. 69 Anderson Street

JAMES GRIFFEN .... 8 Vulcan Street

G.HOLMES........................ Lowry Street/ 98 Short Strand

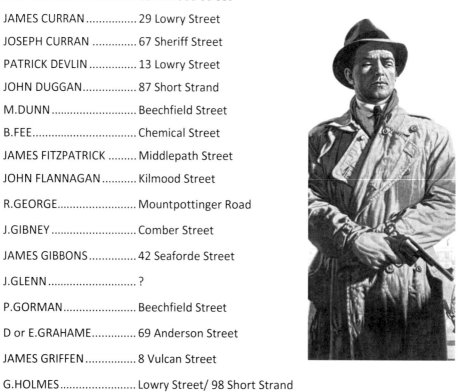

J.HUGHES .... 6 Khartoum Street

C.HUGHES .... 6, Khartoum Street

PATRICK KANE .... 5 Vulcan Street

W.KEARNS .... Thompson Street

KEARNEY .... Lisbon Street

G.IRVINE .... Quinn Street

J.MARLOW .... ?

JAMES MARTIN .... 39 Anderson Street/1 White Street

THOMAS MARTIN .... 39 Anderson Street

H.MOAN .... Mountpottinger Road

T.MOONEY .... Comber Street

J.MUNSTER....................... Seaforde Street

WILLIAM MURRAY .... 66 Chemical Street

A. Mc ALLISTER................. 13 Middlepath Street

MURTAGH Mc ASTOCKER 5 Moira Street

FRANCIS Mc AULEY .... 11 Vulcan Street

J. Mc CAFFREY .... Vulcan Street

WILLIAM Mc CONNELL...............Short Strand/56
                        Anderson Street

JOSEPH Mc DERMOTT...... 49 Kilmood Street

GEORGE Mc GIVERN .... 17 Middlepath Street

HENRY Mc GRATH .... 24 Foundry Street/Youngs Row
[MEGRAW] .... [Went to England]

M.Mc ILLHONE .... Saul Streeet

H. Mc KENNA.................... 79 Foundry Street

W.Mc KENNA .... 79 Foundry Street

JAMES Mc LOUGHLIN....... 11 Foundry Street

C.Mc MANN .... Keenan Street

WILLIAM Mc MENEMY..... 14 Vulcan Street [Went to USA]

GEORGE Mc MULLAN....... 68 Seaforde Street

FRANCIS Mc MULLAN ...... 68 Seaforde Street

R .Mc VEIGH .... ?

E. Mc VITTY...................... Sheriff Street

H. O' HARE...................... [Went to USA]

PATRICK O' NEILL .... Short Strand

DENNIS O' NEILL.............. 29 Short Strand

BERNARD QUINN .... 1 Anderson Street/Mountpottinger Road

T.ROONEY....................... Grahams Place

RICHARD RYAN................ 38 Seaforde Street

WILLIAM SIMPSON........... 94 Bridge End

J.SMITH........................... 36 Beechfield Street

EDWARD STEENSON .... Foundry Street [Went to England]

JAMES THORPE................ 55 Sheriff Street

LEO TOHILL...................... 8 Mountpottinger Road

JOHN WALKER   97 Short Strand

HAMILTON YOUNG .... 11 Foundry Street/Saul Street

NOTE

JAMES FALOONA   3. LOWRY STREET

JOHN STEENSON .... Foundry Street **- *Interned 1922*,** B.Coy ?

JAMES HERON .... Independent Street**, OPERATED WITHIN THE BRIGADE ASU**

Republican Memorial Garden – Ballymacarrett, Short Strand.

Service medal awarded to Volunteer Patrick O'Neill
Picture courtesy of Patrick McCabe

Billy Murray, Left, John Cunningham (centre) at an Old Comrades function late 50s circa
PRONI

Volunteer Murtagh McAstocker, 5 Moira Street
killed on active service 24th September 1921

B COMPANY LISTING - LISTING- 2

VOLUNTEERS NOT LISTED ON THE NOMINAL ROLE AS AT THE PERIOD OF THE TRUCE JULY 1921, BUT JOINED B COMPANY.

THOMAS BYRNE .... 4 Arran Street

PATRICK BURKE .... 91 Bridge End

JIM CLARKE.................................. 8 Vulcan Street

EDWARD COLLINS .... 29 Beechfield Street

PATRICK CROSBIE .... 17 Lowry Street

THOMAS CROSBIE .... 19 Lowry Street

WILLIAM DUGGAN .... 12 Arran Street

HENRY FALOONA .... 53 Seaforde Street

JAMES FALOONA........................... 3 Lowry Street**- Pre truce Volunteer**

MICHAEL FLYNN .... 4 Thompson Street

WILLIAM FRENCH......................... 9 Vulcan Street

MICHAEL GARGIN .... Thompson Place

GEORGE GRAY .... Foundry Street

JOSEPH HOREY .... 38 Comber Street

DANIEL LOUGHRAN...................... 5 Foundry Street

M. MARTIN.................................. 39 Beechfield Street

CHARLES MOONEY........................ 79 Anderson Street

THOMAS MYERS........................... 47 Seaforde Street

DAVID Mc CAVANAGH .... Independent Street

M. J. McCORMICK .... 91 Bridge End

JAMES Mc CRUDDEN .... 9 Seaforde Street

PATRICK Mc MAHON .... 7 Saul Street

WILLIAM McNAMARA.................. 41 Sheriff Street

MICHAEL Mc SHANE .... 10 khartoum Street

GERARD STEELE............................47 Thompson Street

JOHN TOONEY..............................59 Short Strand

JOHN WALSH...............................9 Thompson Street

PHILLIP YOUNG ....5 Khartoum Street

THE FOLLOWING NAMES ARE STILL UNDER RESEARCH AND TO DATE I CAN NOT DEFINITELY CONFIRM AS B. COMPANY, BUT THEY WENT SOUTH FOR TRAINING, EITHER AS 3rd NORTHERN DIVISION, OR TO JOIN THE FREE STATE ARMY.

EDWARD CUNNINGHAM ....40 Clyde Street

WILLIAM DARRAGH ....64 Anderson Street

THOMAS DIXON ....11 Saul Street

THOMAS GORMAN   55 Seaforde Street*

JAMES KANE ....22 Moira Street

JAMES Mc CLELLAND ....37 Arran Street

AARON Mc VITTY ....17 Khartoum Street

JOHN MURPHY.............................36 Clyde Street

A. P. POWER.................................26 Vulcan Street

PATRICK ROONEY.........................43 Kilmood Street

JOHN WOODS ....39 Thompson Street.

*THOMAS GORMAN SERVED IN THE FREE STATE ARMY

I.R.A. FATALITIES

Despite the high casualty listing among the Catholic population in Belfast, the I.R.A. did not suffer
A high ratio loss of men; in fact it was very low. It endured against overwhelming odds.

I.R.A. losses in Belfast were:

Volunteer Seamus Leadie, who died from gunshot wounds in Norfolk Street on the 11th July 1921, the day the truce came into effect.

Volunteer Murtagh McAstocker, of Moira Street Short Strand, who died from gunshot wounds on the Lower Newtownards Road, on 24th September 1921.

Volunteer James Bradley aged 24, who was killed in the battle around York Street/North Queen Street at the end of August 1921. A native of South Derry [where he is buried in Granaghan graveyard] he was working as a Barman in Belfast and living in McCleery Street.

Another South Derry volunteer who died as a result of shooting in Belfast was **John Mc Kenna**. His name is not to be found in the casualty listing, but he died in his home town of Maghera on the 6th July 1921 after being brought home from Belfast. Born in Maghera, he worked in Belfast as a barman, a trade Catholics found work in due to the fact that many of Belfast Public Houses were Catholic owned.

On the 6th February, 1922, **Thomas Gray**, aged 19, who also worked in the bar trade in Boyle's public house of Earl Street, died when gunmen entered the bar and shot him dead.

A week later on the 14th February 1922, **Volunteer Frank Mc Coy**, aged 25, of Forfar Street in the Cavendish Street area was killed near Springfield Avenue.

The following month, on 6th March 1922, **Andrew Leonard**, of Mary Street was shot and wounded by a Loyalist sniper during exchanges of gunfire with the I.R.A. He died seven days later on the 13th March 1922.

IRA FATALITIES

Despite the high casualty listing among the Catholic population in Belfast, the IRA did not suffer a high ratio loss of men; in fact it was very low.
It endured against overwhelming odds.

IRA losses in Belfast were:

Volunteer Seamus Leadie, who died from gunshot wounds in Norfolk Street on the 11th July 1921, the day the truce came into effect.

Volunteer Murtagh Mc Astocker, of Moira Street Short Strand, who died from gunshot wounds on the Lower Newtownards Road, on 24th September 1921.

Volunteer James Bradley aged 24, who was killed in the battle around York Street/North Queen Street at the end of August 1921.
A native of South Derry [where he is buried in *Granaghan* graveyard] he was working as a Barman in Belfast and living in Mc Cleery Street.

Another South Derry volunteer who died as a result of shooting in Belfast was **John Mc Kenna**. His name is not to be found in the casualty listing, but he died in his home town of Maghera on the 6th July 1921 after being brought home from Belfast.

Born in Maghera, he worked in Belfast as a barman, a trade Catholics found work in due to the fact that many of Belfast Public Houses were Catholic owned.

On the 6th February, 1922, **Thomas Gray**, aged 19, who also worked in the bar trade in Boyle's public house of Earl Street, died when gunmen entered the bar and shot him dead.

A week later on the 14th February 1922, **Volunteer Frank Mc Coy,** aged 25, of Forfar Street in the Cavendish Street area was killed near Springfield Avenue.

The following month, on 6th March 1922, **Andrew Leonard,** of Mary Street was shot and wounded by a Loyalist sniper during exchanges of gunfire with the IRA.
He died seven days later on the 13th March 1922.

JOSEPH GILES	20th July 1920	
JOHN Mc FADDEN	26th September 1920	C. COY, 2nd BATTALION
ALEX Mc BRIDE	11th June 1921	SINN FEIN-?
ALEX HAMILTON	11th July 1921	
BERNARD SHANLEY	16th December 1921	
DAVID MORRISON	27th December 1921	
PATRICK FLYNN	? December 1921	
JAMES MORRISON	14th February 1922	
EDWARD Mc KINNEY	24th March 1922	
JAMES Mc GEE	26th March 1922	
JOHN WALKER	20th April 1922	B COY, 2nd BATTALION
WILLIAM THORNTON	18th June 1922	C COY, 2nd BATTALION

It came as no surprise some years ago, that amid Sinn Fein's growing electorical success in the 26 Counties, that Fianna Fail re-established the sub title of "The Republican Party" when touching base with its grass-roots at the party's Ard Fheis.

More recently, [May Day 2013], it again rouses our cynical nature when the Irish Labour Party laid claim to the Starry Plough flag as the centenary of the 1916 Rising looms close.

The party wants to re-assert its claim on one of Ireland's most symbolic flags, designed by Belfast-born artist William H Megahy.

The Labour Party's Barry Desmond commented: *"It was not conceived as a military flag. Its origins was as a flag for the defence of the workers during the 1913 Lockout. It has always been a flag of the Labour Party"*, Mr. Desmond said.

Despite what Mr. Desmond points out, in reality the flag was adopted by the Irish Citizens Army as a "flag of war" and was flown in O'Connell [Sackville] Street during the 1916 rising.

In recent decades, the Labour Party has given greater prominence to the white flag bearing a red rose which is favoured by many EU socialist parties.

But as the centenary of the rising fast approaches, Labour Party Dublin TD, Joe Costello insisted that the Starry Plough belongs to the Labour Party. He stated: *"The Starry Plough is part of our history. We would prefare if others did not use it, but that's not something we can do much about"*.

Mr. Costello further stated: *"The Starry Plough belongs essentially to the Labour and Trade Union Movement."* Perhaps then, based on this assertion from Joe Costello, will we in the near future see the flying of the Starry Plough at Trade Union rallies as an "official" flag, even as a main logo on Trade Union stationery !!!!!!!

As memories and myth collide, old-fashioned rhetoric from 26 county politicians which betray the vision of 1916 and insult the intellect of those who have endeavoured to stay as true as is possible to the principles of republicanism.

In August 2012, Enda Kenny stood at *Beal na Blath* and in typical Finn Gael fashion used the anniversary to spin party policy on the financial state of the country, while his so-called oration lacked class, giving little consideration to the historical occasion.

Collin's actions cast a terrifying shadow of reality over the 26 county state, as do the actions of the IRA during the 1920-1923 periods; the same IRA from which the National [Free State] Army was conceived. *

Moves by the same Finn Gael government to "demilitarise" the 1916 commemorations was evident at Arbour Hill in Dublin during May of this year [2013].

Alan Shatter, the Defence Minister had moved to implement changes to the traditional format of the ceremony involving the 26 county Defence Forces.

A Defence Forces colour party would no longer be present inside the church at the mass or for ceremonially saluting at the Eucharist. Apparently there was even an attempt to remove the army generals from the front row of the church but that was resisted.

The involvement of the Church of Ireland Archbishop of Dublin, Dr. Michael Jackson I would normally view as valuable and certainly one to be welcomed. However, his speech is worth noting when he said:

"T his generation of Irish people should be cautious of those who politically manipulate and exploit the legacy of 1916 and surrounding events." [Perhaps he should have given a little glance in the direction of Alan Shatter!]

The Archbishop continued: *"History develops a new function, that of releasing new energy in a tired and repetitive world, porous to exploitation by those who know that old fears and old symbols still sell and who still suppress those who think otherwise and think for themselves."* [In other words, the sooner we revise our history the better]

The symptoms of this governments unease with 1916 was no more apparent when the presidential wreath was laid in memory not just of the executed leaders but for all those who died around the events of 1916. [Presumably, this includes British forces that died putting down the rising]

It is three years to 2016 and the centenary and if this is the path the 26 county state has embarked on, then the revisionist script-writers are already burning the midnight oil.

Perhaps the nervousness rippling through Finn Gael in the run up to 2016 is driven by a need to reinvent our past. Some 97 years after 1916, do they still feel it is not safe for us to be left loose with our own history, warts, guns and all!

One could not be faulted for thinking that there is a whole generation within the 26 counties, who are of the mindset that the only blood spilled was in movies, that war with all its cold overtures and terrible sadness "happened in the north" in recent times and they live in a State immune to such things. *

I wait with anticipation at how the southern government intend facing the civil war period when that centenary comes to cast it's dark shadow. In the meantime they may also want to start taking a close look at the ruthless *but effective* tactics of Michael Collins in the road toward the Independence they have gravely abused. *

In the north, Sinn Fein and the mainstream Republican Movement need to be careful that in their quest to "*manage*" the history of our recent conflict, they do not end up emulating the De Valera period of the thirties and forties restricting it to use as a political tool. *

No one has the right to claim ownership of what belongs to all of our people and condemn the right to voice dissent. Personal ambition can lead to tunnel vision and that in turn distracts from focusing on the true and rightful objectives. *

It is easy to accuse those who think our past conflict needs to be properly addressed as "not moving forward." The Good Friday agreement, which I like many, supported with some apprehension, appears to have been formatted in such a haphazard manner, it has been left open to a contradiction of expectations. *

If you can not deliver proper cohesive policy, then you are failing; tolerance does not meet expectation, it simply prolongs the frustration. *

History is a strong component; it can judge or condemn, but equally guide and lead us.*

The history of our recent conflict puts an onus on all of us to take ownership-It is OUR history**, it does not belong to the many, or the few, but to ALL of us. ***

It should not be revised and used as a political tool, nor should it be denied. We can learn, challenge and be guided, not only from the actions which we considered as morally right, but from the mistakes that can often be so easily made with good intention. *

Sean O'Coinn   JUNE 2013

SOURCES: Sean O'Coinn-Belfast   *

Sunday Independent - Jody Corcoran 26th August 2013

Irish Daily Mail - Tom Mc Gurk 11th May 2013

Irish News -1st May 2013

Sean O'Coinn is a Belfast based Author and Historian and a former Republican activist. He has written several books and numerous articles on contemporary Irish history.